Two Plays by
Victor L. Cahn

*To Julia
Fondly, Vic*

www.stagerights.com

A DISH FOR THE GODS
Copyright © 2013 by Victor L. Cahn
All Rights Reserved

SHEEPSKIN
Copyright © 1999 by Victor L. Cahn
All Rights Reserved

All performances and public readings of A DISH FOR THE GODS and SHEEPSKIN are subject to royalties. It is fully protected under the copyright laws of the United States of America, of all countries covered by the International Copyright Union, of all countries covered by the Pan-American Copyright Convention and the Universal Copyright Convention, and all countries with which the United States has reciprocal copyright relations. All rights are strictly reserved.

No part of this book may be reproduced, stored in a retrieval system, or transmitted in any form, by any means, including mechanical, electronic, photocopying, recording, or otherwise, without the prior written permission of the author. Publication of this play does not necessarily imply that it is available for performance by amateurs or professionals. It is strongly recommended all interested parties apply to Steele Spring Stage Rights for performance rights before starting rehearsals or advertising.

No changes shall be made in the play for the purpose of your production without prior written consent. All billing stipulations in your license agreement must be strictly adhered to. No person, firm or entity may receive credit larger or more prominent than that accorded the Author.

For all stage performance inquiries, please contact:

Steele Spring Stage Rights
3845 Cazador Street
Los Angeles, CA 90065
(323) 739-0413

www.stagerights.com

A WORD FROM THE AUTHOR

I've spent my professional life, forty-five years' worth, in school. During that time I've always written plays, but only two have been set in the world I've come to know so well.

Here they are.

Both are two-handers about a middle-aged, male professor of English and a younger, female student.

Both originated in forms other than their current one: *A Dish for the Gods* began as a dramatic monologue, while *Sheepskin* was initially a three-character, one-act piece.

The salient distinction between the two is tone. *A Dish for the Gods* acknowledges certain follies of academic life, but more importantly dramatizes the powerful and positive influence a teacher may exert. I've labeled *Sheepskin* "a farce noir," because while it giddily mocks undergraduate and graduate existence, it has a dark undercurrent.

Given my own time as an instructor in English, readers may wonder if either of these stories is based on personal experience.

No.

Indeed, all four characters are fictional, but I confess that they do reflect aspects of people I've known. And while the plots are imaginary, they invoke struggles that I've witnessed, and that as yet endure.

These plays were also written many years apart. *A Dish for the Gods* was produced Off-Broadway in 2013, and *Sheepskin* was originally presented there in 1982. Some thematic elements are common to both, but others reflect the time of creation. In particular, over the decades the role of women has altered profoundly, and I believe that these scripts reflect such progress.

Still, what pleases me most about them is that their impact springs from the reality of the academic universe. Such an environment is often dismissed as dramatically arid, but I hope these plays demonstrate that conflicts on campus, especially between teachers and students, are ripe with theatrical possibility.

Victor L. Cahn

www.stagerights.com

PRODUCTION HISTORY

The world premiere of A DISH FOR THE GODS was produced by Rachel Reiner Productions, LLC at the Lion Theatre @ Theatre Row in New York City on September 16, 2013. The Director was Adam Fitzgerald, the Set Designer was David Arsenault, the Costume Designer was Brooke Cohen, the Lighting Designer was Nastassia Jimenez, the Sound Designer was Colin Whitely, and the Stage Manager was Sean McCain. The cast was as follows:

Julia .... MARGOT WHITE
Greg .... KEVIN CRISTALDI

SUMMARY

A celebrated author recounts memorable moments from her surprising life:
the challenges she faced, the choices she made, and the singular man she loved.

CHARACTERS

JULIA: 45-50. Elegant, witty.
GREG: Several years older than Julia. Handsome, dynamic.

SCENE

The Place: A lecture hall
The Time: The present
The play is performed without intermission.

SETTING

A lectern (preferably on wheels) is placed prominently. A table (also preferably on wheels) and two chairs, as well as benches at RIGHT and LEFT, may be used to represent various locales.

COSTUMES

JULIA wears a suit, sheer stockings, and pumps.
GREG wears a jacket, a shirt, jeans, and loafers, and may change accouterments.

ACT I

VOICEOVER

Welcome to A DISH FOR THE GODS. Please take a minute to silence all cell phones and electronic devices.
>*(a beat)*

Thank you for your patience. I am at last delighted to introduce our guest for this evening: an eminent writer and lecturer and a national ambassador for the arts. You know her from many appearances on television and radio… and she is just now entering the hall. Would you please welcome… Julia Reynolds.

>*JULIA, carrying a travel bag, hurries onstage from the house.*

JULIA
>*(to the audience)*

Thanks for waiting! I am so sorry!

>*As SHE gathers herself, SHE acknowledges whatever applause is forthcoming.*

Thank you so much! I have to tell you. I had a rough time getting here. First my flight was delayed two hours. Then the security system malfunctioned, and everyone had to go through twice. That's when a woman with that electronic wand felt compelled to examine every inch of my body so closely that I figured she had to be the airport gynecologist.
>*(a beat)*

Finally during the taxi ride over, my driver got lost, and I had to provide directions. Not easy because I've never been here. In other words, I need a breather.

>*SHE finds a bottle near the lectern and down a drink.*

Water. Not exactly what I had in mind, but I'll take it.

>*SHE takes another swallow.*

Oh, by the way.

>*SHE takes a deep breath.*

Good-evening-thank-you-very-much-for-that-kind-introduction-I-didn't-hear-all-of-it-but-I'm-sure-it-was-very-generous-what-a-charming-town-you-have-and-what-a-lovely-building.

>*SHE exhales.*

Actually, I wasn't sure I'd be able to make it tonight. But when someone as distinguished as your chairwoman invites me to speak about books and women and writing, and especially about women who write books, how can I refuse? I won't reveal how long ago we met, but this suit was still in style.
>*(a beat)*

Well… enough excuses.

> *SHE picks up her travel bag and removes several papers.*

JULIA (CONT'D)
Down to business.

> *SHE places the pages on the lectern and the bag on the floor.*

Let me begin by mentioning a few names. See how many you recognize.
> *(She reads)*

Daisy Ashford.
> *(a beat)*

Mary Webb.
> *(a beat)*

Sarah Grand. Marjorie Firminger. Vera Brittain.
> *(a beat, to the audience)*

I'm not hearing any mumbles of recognition. I'm not surprised.
> *(a beat, to the audience)*

Who are they? Well, all were women. All were British. All lived in the late nineteenth to mid-twentieth centuries. All were writers. And all are forgotten. What happened? Nothing complicated. They were lost in the critical shuffle.
> *(a beat)*

Such has been the fate of too many gifted women. I'm not including the myriad others whose talents lay forever dormant, crushed by some combination of domestic responsibility, societal and marital constriction, and the indifference or outright antagonism of the male literary establishment. And if those talents did manage to break through, most had to do so without the patronage, financial and otherwise, that all artists need if they're going to… flourish.
> *(short pause)*

Excuse me.

> *JULIA turns to the lectern and looks at notes.*

Even today, when women writers have proven that their efforts deserve to be regarded as more than "women's work," they still struggle to make their voices resound.
> *(a beat)*

And that's the subject I want to discuss with you tonight. How we can release that… that latent force within us…
> *(a beat)*

I'm sorry.
> *(short pause)*

I've delivered several versions of this presentation. Right now, however, I find myself at a loss…

JULIA (CONT'D)
(short pause)

Let me try a different approach.

SHE shuffles pages.

Has anyone heard of Violet Hunt?

(a beat)

She was a novelist and feminist from that same period. She was deeply admired by Oscar Wilde, who may have proposed marriage. And we know how remarkable a possibility *that* had to be. Years later she became involved with other writers, including the eminent novelist Ford Madox Ford, as well as H.G. Wells. And when I say "involved," I trust you understand what I mean.

(a beat)

She was apparently quite a sexual predator. D.H. Lawrence met her just once and proclaimed her to be "a real assassin."

SHE shuffles pages.

She was also... also the model for characters in famous books by various... authors...

(pause)

My apologies. I thought I could bring this off, but I seem to have overestimated my ability to deal with some recent remarkable circumstances. Don't worry. My health is excellent. Nevertheless, I find myself unsettled.

SHE moves the lectern aside.

This is going to be off the cuff, so please forgive any awkwardness.

(a beat)

I'll start this way. When you hear me rattle off these names, you may assume I'm something of a scholar. Well, don't be too impressed. I'm not saying I'm bad. I'm just admitting that I'm far from the best.

(a beat)

The more important point is that I came to it all rather late, because even though I'm the product of two high-powered parents, an attorney (my father) and a dermatologist (my mother), for a long time I wasn't much of a student. Maybe I was subconsciously rebelling against all their propaganda about finding my place in the world.

(a beat)

Whatever my feelings, I survived high school and was accepted to college, but I didn't want to go, and I certainly didn't have any plans for when I arrived. Still, all my friends were taking that route, so I followed.

(a beat)

It didn't work out, because I couldn't care about my classes. I didn't blame myself. My professors simply bored me, so in the middle of my third year, after wallowing to excess in the social trough, I quit.

JULIA (CONT'D)
(a beat)

Over my parents' objections, I took a job answering the phone in a plumbing firm. There I spent most of my time fending off the sniffs and gropes of both labor and management.

(a beat)

For a while I was a waitress, but I couldn't abide customers who snapped their fingers to get my attention. What pushed me over the edge was a family of six, who left a two percent tip under a plate of vomited vegetables.

(a beat)

I also worked in a dry cleaner. Until then I had sort of liked clothes, but after wading through thousands of laundry bags filled with the assorted smells and stains of underwear, towels, socks, shirts, and sheets, apparel in any form lost its allure.

(a beat)

Eventually circumstances brought me to the wilds of southern Pennsylvania, where I found a position in the Registrar of Blanton University. Seven years had passed since I had quit school, but here I was again, although an employee, not a student.

(a beat)

My job required that I track enrollments, collect grades, and compile transcripts. Nothing thrilling, but after my other employment, the civilized veneer of academia was reassuring.

One of the perks of my post was campus gossip, usually supplied by students eager to spill the beans about their professors. Here's where I first heard the name "Greg Davidson." He was thirty-five and a member of the English Department. Newly tenured, and thus assured of a lifetime position, he was a faculty fireball, whose classrooms overflowed with students. He rushed around campus, always in the midst of conversation. He usually wore a tweed jacket, a blue shirt (unbuttoned at the top), and jeans. Outside, in even the bitterest cold, he added only a scarf. His mouth was sensuously full. His hair was perpetually windswept. And if it wasn't, he made sure to sweep it.

(a beat)

His office corridor was inevitably packed with students seeking his pronouncements on even the most personal aspects of their lives. Meanwhile his colleagues sat alone in their own cubby holes, stewing.

(a beat)

He frequented local bars: smoking, drinking, and exchanging subversive opinions with denizens full of nicotine, liquor, and themselves. He was single and... how can I put this... energetic.

(a beat)

I know what you're thinking. I was in my late twenties, unmarried, and as receptive to male charm as any giddy teenager. Maybe. But he *was* special.

JULIA (CONT'D)
(a beat)

Whenever he submitted grades or other rigmarole, he tended to burst in long after whatever deadline had been imposed, then grandly deposit materials.

GREG enters.

GREG
(to the audience)

Ladies, good afternoon! A delight to see you all, and no doubt you will be thrilled to learn that I come bearing gifts.

JULIA
(to the audience)

His attitude ensured that whatever inconvenience he created was immediately forgiven. He also rarely left without a casual exchange or two.

GREG
(to the audience)

I have to put new tiles in my kitchen floor. Does anybody know the best place?

JULIA
(to the audience)

Or...

GREG
(to the audience)

Did you see that game last night? Triple overtime.
(a beat)
What were you doing instead?
(a beat)
Oh. With your husband, I hope.

HE sits.

JULIA
(to the audience)

Naturally I wanted to know him better, so I resolved to observe him in his native habitat: the classroom. That's when I called his office.

GREG
Davidson here. Who's there?

JULIA
Hi, Greg. It's Julia Reynolds from the Registrar.

GREG
Hey! How ya' doin'?

JULIA
Fine, thanks.

GREG
Great! What's up?
JULIA
Well, I wanted to ask you–
GREG
Uh-oh. Now I'm nervous.
JULIA
Why?
GREG
Because I must have done something wrong to warrant a call from so exalted a personage.
JULIA
Not at all–
GREG
Did I lose a form? Drop fifty kids from a course?
JULIA
No–
GREG
Give a whole class an incomplete?
JULIA
(laughing)
Nothing like that. I swear!
GREG
Thank God! What can I do for you?
JULIA
Well, I wanted to ask a favor.
GREG
Anything I can do.
JULIA
Thanks. Actually, the thing is… I've heard a lot about your classes.
GREG
Lies. All lies.
JULIA
So I was wondering if you wouldn't mind if some morning I… uhhh… sat in.
GREG
That's it?
JULIA
That's it.

GREG

Absolutely. Any time.

JULIA

Should I call first?

GREG

Don't bother. Just take a seat. I don't mean carry it outside…

JULIA
(laughing)

I know. You're sure it's no trouble?

GREG

Door's always open.

GREG leaves.

JULIA
(to the audience)

A week later, I walked into a lecture hall with approximately two hundred seats, all but a few occupied. The performance that followed was unlike anything I had ever seen. The course was "World Drama," and the subject was *The Taming of the Shrew*, Shakespeare's iconic battle of the sexes.
(a beat)
You probably know the plot: about the bitter Kate and her suitor, the lusty Petruchio. The two initially clash, but after he takes her home, then denies her food and sleep for a night, their wrangling evolves into amorous banter. The play concludes with Kate's urging other women to find happiness by pleasing their husbands.
(a beat)
Some critics, especially those of a feminist bent, have accused Shakespeare of sanctioning the suppression of a spirited woman.

GREG enters.

GREG
(to the audience)

Morning, gang!

JULIA
(to the audience)

Greg, however, interpreted the action differently.

JULIA leaves the playing area.

GREG
(to the audience)

They're missing the point! Petruchio's not brutalizing her! He's compelling her to tear off what he knows is a mask that disguises her unhappiness. He's not cruel. He simply senses her capacity for love that's been hidden under her antagonism for the pathetic males of Padua!

GREG (CONT'D)
(a beat)

And how does Petruchio know this? Because he feels the same desolation, and he spends the bulk of the play teaching Kate that lesson.
(a beat)

But let's be more specific. What do these two characters, particularly Kate, actually learn? Not just that they love each other, but that happiness in any relationship, especially marriage, belongs to those who surrender a portion of themselves for mutual happiness. That's the heart of Kate's famous last address.
(a beat)

And what is the pervasive irony of this play? That although these characters constantly quarrel, the play is a comedy. And conventions of the theater, at least in Shakespeare's day, guarantee that no matter how painful the trials that Kate and Petruchio endure, the pair must resolve their squabbles in marriage. Remember, Shakespeare's contemporaries prized order, and they viewed marriage as its bedrock.
(a beat)

Now, where do we go from here? Why does all this matter to us?
(a beat)

Because like these "madly mated lovers," you and I wander through existence desperate for meaning. Only we do so without the benefit of an audience watching with god-like assurance that all will resolve happily.

JULIA
(to the audience)

Mixed in with these grand concepts were references to television and movies, sports and politics, philosophy and music. The overall impact was something like…

GREG
(to the audience)

I'm thinking of Hitchcock's *North by Northwest*, and the matter of Roger Thornhill/George Kaplan's ever-shifting identity. I'm thinking of Don Quixote and Jay Gatsby, and their doomed attempts at the creation of self. I'm thinking of Dostoevsky's Raskolnikov, The Book of Job, and Wagner's Wotan, especially in *Die Walküre*, all of which dramatize the challenge of determining one's own fate. I'm thinking of Sergeant Bilko, the quintessential American trickster of the 1950s. And I'm thinking of Laurel and Hardy. Not because they have anything to do with the play. Just that thoughts of Stan and Ollie always make me happy.
(a beat)

Some of you might not recognize every one of these allusions, but trust me. They're all brilliant.

GREG leaves. JULIA returns to the playing area.

JULIA
(to the audience)
Did *anyone* in the room recognize every one of those references? Probably not. Did they all make sense? Probably not. Did anyone care? Definitely not.
(a beat)
What mattered was his ecstatic presentation, the rare sort of spectacle that lifts college students out of their customary torpor. It lifted me, too.
(a beat)
At the time I was twelve courses short of a bachelor's degree. But after seeing Greg in action, I was ready to start again, so I signed up for his spring class in Expository Writing. The group included fifteen other students, eleven of them female, every one a decade younger than I and annoyingly adorable.
(a beat)
The course was structured around individual conferences, so after the first two classes, during which I sat silently, Greg and I met in his office: a mélange of books, papers, journals and coffee cups. Our task was to review my first essay, a narrative about working for the Registrar.

GREG enters and sits in one of the chairs. JULIA walks to him.

JULIA
Hi, Professor Davidson.

GREG
Professor Davidson! Are you kidding? You've been calling me by my first name since day one. Besides, we're from the same generation, so if you don't call me "Greg," I'll feel ancient.

JULIA
"Greg" it is.

GREG
Good. Have a seat.

SHE sits. HE holds up several pages.

GREG (CONT'D)
Your paper, in case you don't recognize it.

JULIA
Looks familiar.

GREG
Good.
(a beat)
What do you think of it?

JULIA
I like it, I guess.

GREG
Hmmm. You do?
JULIA
Shouldn't I?
GREG
I'm not sure. I do see promise.
JULIA
That's good.
GREG
But I think there's something fundamentally wrong with it.
JULIA
Oh. That's bad.
GREG
Any idea what I mean?
JULIA
Not really.
GREG
Okay. Tell you what. I'm going to read it out loud. When you think you realize what might be wrong, stop me.

GREG reads and scribbles on the paper.

JULIA
(to the audience)
I didn't expect that hearing my own words would be fun, but the process soon became excruciating, because Greg kept pausing to mark errors. A third of the way through, he stopped.
GREG
See what's wrong yet?
JULIA
I've made a lot of mistakes.
GREG
Obviously, but that's not important now. Let's keep going.
JULIA
(to the audience)
I sensed condescension, but I stayed calm. As he read further, he found more errors that he indicated in red pen.

GREG writes more violently.

JULIA (CONT'D)
(to the audience)
The paper looked as if someone had been bleeding on it.

GREG

Well?

JULIA

Maybe I haven't organized my ideas effectively.

GREG

You haven't, but that's not the big problem, either. Anything else come to mind?

JULIA

No.

GREG

Okay. Let's finish it.

JULIA
(to the audience)

And he did, in a snail-like pace that left me incensed.

HE finishes correcting with a flourish.

GREG

What do you think now? What's wrong?

JULIA
(to the audience)

Never in my life had I felt so feeble.
(To GREG)
I don't know what's wrong! That's why I'm in the class!

GREG

Right. Well, do you want to write another draft?

JULIA

I don't know. Do I?

GREG

I don't know. Do you?

JULIA

I don't know!

GREG

I don't, either.

JULIA

Then what should I do?

GREG

Why don't you want to write it over?

JULIA

Look, if you want me to, I'll do it.

GREG
Do you want to?
JULIA
Not really.
GREG
Why not?
JULIA
I don't know!
(short pause)
Maybe because it's sort of–
GREG
What?
(a beat)
Sort of what?
JULIA
I don't... know.
GREG
I think I do.
JULIA
Then would you please tell me?
GREG
Sure. The reason you don't want to write it over is that it's... BORING!
JULIA
What?
GREG
It's DULL, and it's LIFELESS, and it's BORING! Am I right?
JULIA
I don't know–
GREG
Am I right?
JULIA
I guess so–
GREG
Of course I'm right! As my mother used to say, it's dull as dishwater.
(short pause)
Tell me honestly. Are you really interested in sending out transcripts?
JULIA
No.

GREG

Do you care remotely about Ellen Macklin and her trip to a chicken farm?

JULIA

No.

GREG

So what do we do?

JULIA

I don't know!

GREG

We do this!

HE rips the pages into pieces.

GREG (CONT'D)

I don't care about this essay. Because you didn't care about it when you wrote it.

JULIA

Excuse me–

GREG

You wasted your time, and you wasted mine.

JULIA

I beg your pardon!

GREG

Yes?

JULIA

I spent five and a half hours on this paper–

GREG

And you wasted every minute.

HE takes her hand and puts the torn pages in it. SHE stares at the remnants.

JULIA

Do I at least get a grade?

GREG

It's not worth a grade.

JULIA

(to the audience)

I wanted to kill him. I wanted him dead on the floor.

GREG

As I was saying, what do we do?

JULIA

And as I was saying, I don't know!

SHE sits. Pause.

GREG

Why don't you pick a better topic?

JULIA

Okay.

Pause.

GREG

Up to me, huh?

(a beat)

All right. Let me ask you something. Is there anyone or anything that at this moment you really hate? I mean, besides me.

Short pause.

JULIA

A few years ago I worked in a law office.

GREG

Go on.

JULIA

You asked if I hated something.

GREG

And you hated that?

JULIA

Oh, yeah.

GREG

Why?

JULIA

The lawyers were arrogant, the pay was lousy, the people were cold—

GREG

Sounds like the Blanton English Department. Good. Write about it. Make me hate it, too. Okay?

HE smiles.

Thanks for dropping by.

HE resumes working.

JULIA

(to the audience)

When I left, I was still angry, but I was also determined to show him what I could do. So I went home and wrote furiously. Three days later, I brought another essay.

GREG holds a different paper.

GREG

I hope I'll find lots of hate here.

JULIA

You will.

SHE sits.
(to the audience)

I was relieved that he didn't tear it up. Not literally. But he corrected it with the same intensity.

HE hands the paper to her.

GREG

Now you're cooking.

JULIA

Is it better?

GREG

That's a bit strong, but it's a start.
(a beat)
Yes, it's better. But I need more detail. Sights, smells, sounds. Everywhere I circled. Can you do it?

JULIA

I think so.

GREG

I know so.

JULIA
(to the audience)

I rewrote it again, and he corrected it again. And I rewrote again. And he corrected again. Each time he forced me to check transitions, unify paragraphs, and cut useless verbiage. He refused to accept sloppy logic. He challenged me in every way, and before long I was tougher on myself than he was.
(to Greg)
I hate making so many mistakes! I feel as if I'm still wasting time.

GREG

You blundered, right?

JULIA

Right.

GREG

But you know what you did wrong.

JULIA

Now I do.

GREG

Then you learned something.

JULIA

Right.

GREG

Then you're not wasting your time.

JULIA
(to the audience)

I wrote piece after piece about my family, my jobs, and various social and political issues. My writing grew crisp and tight. And when I submitted my final paper…

GREG

Terrific. And if it matters to you, I'd give it an A.

JULIA
(to the audience)

He also added one more comment.

GREG

You're finding your own voice.

HE leaves.

JULIA
(to the audience)

I melted.

(a beat)

Let me be clear. That course changed my life. For the first time, I learned for the sheer satisfaction, even the joy, of doing so. The grade pleased me, but it really didn't matter. At last I wanted to do something. I imagined myself as a teacher, a writer… *something.* A fire burned inside me. You know who lit the flame.

(a beat)

I continued working for my degree, which included a major in English and more courses with Greg. Between my classes and my job I was exhausted, but happy. I also earned A's in every class. Except one: Early American Literature.

(a beat)

The problem was the professor, a troglodyte in a turtleneck. He resented all women, but especially what he called "uppity females." Maybe that's why he taught books about burning witches or branding women with scarlet letters. Anyway, he disliked me on sight, probably because I was older and less vulnerable to intimidation. He also knew that I was close to Greg, whom he hated.

              JULIA (CONT'D)
              (a beat)
He gave my first paper a D minus (the minus was gratuitously nasty), and attacked the work so viciously that as women often do, I began to believe the worst: that my writing was, in his words, "pointless and pedestrian."
                    GREG enters.
              JULIA (CONT'D)
              (to the audience)
In desperation I showed the paper to Greg.
              GREG
It's fine. Worth an A.
              JULIA
But what about his corrections? Is he right about anything?
              GREG
Sure. You spelled "supersede" wrong. Twice. Otherwise you're okay.
              JULIA
But what about–
              GREG
Listen. Look what you're doing in this paper. You're exalting the courage and intellect of women characters. As well as their sexual power. My favorite part, by the way.
                HE smiles. So does JULIA.
              GREG (CONT'D)
He doesn't want to read that stuff. So forget about him. But prepare yourself, because you're going to run into plenty of guys like him who don't want you to succeed. I do.
                       HE leaves.
              JULIA
              (to the audience)
Buttressed by his encouragement, I gobbled up courses, so by the next summer I was ready to graduate. But I wasn't finished. I applied for a fellowship to join the Blanton Master's degree program in English. I was accepted, and the award enabled me to quit my job and study full-time.
              (a beat)
Long before that adventure, however, complications had set in.
              (short pause)
I have to go back a little. At the end of that first writing course, Greg invited me to lunch. It was all public and respectable.
              (a beat)
Weeks later, at his invitation, I accompanied him to his favorite hangout, the Eastcheap Tavern, named after Falstaff's place of business in Shakespeare's *Henry IV*, and where I joined a circle of Greg's acolytes.

JULIA (CONT'D)
Like the fat knight himself, Greg presided over ribald banter that encompassed art, politics, life, love, and the pursuit of happiness. The laughter was constant, but to my mind everybody was trying too hard to show what a good time they were having. After midnight, the revelry moved to Greg's house, a two-story frame structure a few blocks from downtown. The living room was decorated with a hodgepodge of furniture covered with books and papers, bottles and glasses. It was as if his office had been transplanted. Greg held court in a giant leather lounger.
(a beat, to the audience)
I stayed until two in the morning. By the time I left, the remaining figures included three girls lying supine and barefoot. All were insensate, and two had disposed of their blouses and bras. The other survivor was a boy who stood rotating his head in synchronization with a record spinning soundlessly on a turntable. Was this how Greg spent his life outside school? I hadn't experienced such a gathering since my undergraduate days. Something in this spectacle struck me as ineffably sad.

GREG enters and sits at the table.

JULIA (CONT'D)
(to the audience)
Even so, when Greg asked me to supper out of town, I agreed. That night our conversation turned from me and my work to him and his, and after the first round of drinks, he let loose, talking more to himself than to me.

SHE sits with him.

GREG
I have all these projects to finish. A history of American drama. Articles. Even a novel. But I can't get to them. I feel my life slipping away.
(a beat)
Writers have to be selfish. Remember what William Faulkner said: the "Ode on a Grecian Urn" is worth any number of little old ladies.
(a beat)
Teaching comes easily to me, because I have the talent to spew entertaining nonsense. But writing means plugging away, alone, one sentence at a time. And even if I squeeze out a few lines, that doesn't mean they're worth anything.

JULIA
But you're a phenomenal teacher.

GREG
Compared to what? The rest of the faculty? They can't draw flies!

JULIA
The students worship you.

GREG
What do they know?

JULIA
You own this campus.
GREG
Look, I admit I have fun showing off, and rolling from one audience to another. And I'm good at it.
JULIA
You're great at it.
GREG
But so what? Students walk in one door and out the other. And in the end, their opinion doesn't matter one damn bit.
JULIA
You shape people's lives!
GREG
And what does that get *me*?
JULIA
What more do you want?
GREG
In this business you become somebody by writing. I'm not doing any.
JULIA
You once told me, and I quote, nobody reads that academic garbage.
GREG
They don't.
JULIA
And you said you have no interest in appealing to pompous windbags.
GREG
I don't.
JULIA
Then why do you care?
(to the audience)
He couldn't answer, but you know what I felt like asking: if he wanted to write, why did he throw away so many nights at the Eastcheap? But I knew why. Bloviating in a bar was a lot easier than working.
GREG leaves.
(to the audience)
I also realized something else. To his legion of fans, including me, part of Greg's appeal was his scorn for what used to be called "the establishment": his Department, the University administration, most figures of authority. Nothing gave us more gratification than hearing him mock these people. Yet he was also desperate that they take him seriously. As much as he disdained the big shots, that's how much he craved their approval. No wonder he was in torment.

JULIA (CONT'D)
(a beat)

During the meal he drank nonstop. Afterwards, I dropped him off at his house, and watched him stagger inside.
(a beat)

It's always a shock to realize that your teacher is a human being. That night Greg's self-loathing was on full display. Even worse, and I hate saying so, seeing him in such condition made me feel better about myself.
(short pause)

After that, Greg began to hint none too subtly that he wanted our relationship to move to the next level. So did I, but I resisted both our impulses until officially we were no longer student and teacher.

GREG enters.

JULIA (CONT'D)
(to the audience)

Then on a steamy June night, we went to the Eastcheap, ate a leisurely meal, and drank much too much.

THEY sit close together.

GREG

You look particularly lovely tonight.

JULIA

Thank you.

GREG

In fact, if it's not too sexist, I'd say you're what I'd call "a dish."

JULIA

I'm flattered.

GREG

Although you might prefer "a dish for the gods." That's from *Antony and Cleopatra*.

JULIA

Spoken by... ?

GREG

The character is never named. He's called simply "clown," he appears at the very end with the notorious basket of snakes, and he's referring obliquely to the queen herself.

JULIA

I'm impressed.

GREG

You mean, that I remember such details even in my post-prandial haze.

JULIA

No. That you almost make it sound as though you've never said it to a woman before.

Short pause.

GREG

You realize that it's been years since I've met anyone as fascinating as you.

JULIA

I don't believe that, either. But keep talking.

THEY kiss.

GREG

Interested in dessert?

JULIA

Not here.

SHE walks away.
(to the audience)

Somehow we got back to his place. The air conditioner was broken, so we sweated like crazy.

SHE kicks off her shoes.

GREG

We come now to the master bedroom…

SHE hurries to kiss him passionately. THEY sit close together. SHE lays her legs across his.

JULIA
(to the audience)

… where what happened was quite extraordinary. He had a way of tracing my face with his fingers. A lot of men do that, but as his eyes stared deep into mine, and his body lay close, the move worked. He also didn't rush. I was surprised, because in class everything was bang, bang. So to speak. But here he took his time. Eventually he wrapped me in his arms and fell asleep.

HE kisses her, then leaves.

JULIA (CONT'D)
(to the audience)

For a while I remained awake. I thought back to the first time I had seen him teach, when he had seemed a remote, even romantic, figure. Now I was drifting off in his embrace.

(a beat)

My reverie darkened when I remembered that initial orgy, which began at the Eastcheap and concluded in his living room. But I assured myself that when he found the right partner, such antics would fade.

JULIAN (CONT'D)
She would be the beneficiary of all his passions, and her presence would alleviate his gloomier moods. And right then, with his smell and touch enveloping me, I imagined how I might be that partner.
(a beat)
The memory of that moment still leaves me breathless.
(pause)
Greg once claimed that two sensual pleasures unique to womanhood are strutting in a pair of high heels, then kicking off those heels. His tone was paternalistic, but he was right. Unfortunately, decorum demands a certain dignity, so...

SHE puts on her shoes.
(to the audience)

That fall I started courses for my Master's degree. As part of my fellowship, I taught for the first time: World Lit 101. And now *I* was lecturing on *The Taming of the Shrew*, and love, sharing, and mutual support. I enjoyed being the object of all those eyes, and a large part of the fun was playing with ideas in front of a crowd. Do I remind you of anyone?
(a beat)
Greg didn't teach in the graduate program, so I couldn't take more classes with him. Still, we were together a lot. I tried to be discreet, because I didn't want to be known as "his girl." That's why I kept my own apartment. That's also why I stayed away from his office. I wasn't pleased by the attention he devoted to students, particularly female ones, but that's who he was. So when we wanted to be alone, really alone, we went out of town. First we took a couple of weekends, then a ten-day vacation.
(a beat)
I loved those times. Away from Blanton, he was less flamboyant, almost modest. I don't remember a cross word between us.

GREG enters.

JULIA (CONT'D)
(to the audience)

I do remember driving past a new housing complex a few miles outside town.

GREG
These places should be terrific. Porches, big yards. Perfect for bringing up a family.

JULIA
Are you suggesting... ?

GREG
Take it any way you want.

A beat.

JULIA
You want children?
GREG
You sound surprised.
JULIA
You?
GREG
Why not me?
JULIA
They take a lot of time, you know.
GREG
I know.
JULIA
And attention. And devotion.
GREG
What's your point?

A beat.

JULIA
You?

GREG walks away.

JULIA (CONT'D)
(to the audience)
I let the subject slide. But it never strayed far from my mind.
(short pause)
To reciprocate for his help with my writing, I offered to read some of his.

SHE walks to him.

I didn't set myself up as an authority, just a sympathetic audience.
GREG
It's not ready yet.
JULIA
(to Greg)
Not even a peek?
GREG
I'm still refining, restructuring–
JULIA
C'mon!
GREG
NO!

HE leaves.

JULIA
(to the audience)
That was the first time he became angry.
(a beat)
I doubted that he was writing at all. Should I have encouraged him, the way he had motivated me? Maybe. But I didn't. I felt pressure to finish my work and get on with my life. Besides, suppose he was trying, but failing. My intrusion might have given his ego a beating. And where would that have left me? And us? So I let him drift, convincing myself that he'd find his way.
(a beat)
Does that explanation sound weak? Did I owe Greg the same commitment he had given me?
(short pause)
Then IT happened: one of those unexpected turns in the road that leaves a life upside down. The metaphors are mixed, but you know what I mean.
(a beat)
For a couple of years, Greg had hosted a talk show on local public radio. In April, Liz Conrad, editor of the feminist press Womanbooks in New York City, was a scheduled guest.

GREG enters.

JULIA (CONT'D)
(to the audience)
Greg was not looking forward to the interview.

GREG
I have no interest in listening to her rant about matters gynecoid.

JULIA
(to the audience)
Great word, isn't it? "Gynecoid." Means "relating to women."

GREG
Why don't you take it?

JULIA (CONT'D)
(to the audience)
I grabbed it.

GREG leaves. SHE sits at the table.

JULIA (CONT'D)
(to the audience)
I was nervous, but came in with a series of provocative questions, and the show went beautifully. Right away I discovered that one of life's underappreciated treats is talking into a studio microphone. On that strange platform, I felt free, and ideas flowed out of me. I'm not saying they were particularly clever. They just flowed.

JULIA (CONT'D)
(a beat)

After the interview, I mentioned that I was writing my Master's thesis on the aforementioned Violet Hunt, and Liz asked when I anticipated finishing. "Over the summer," I said. "Fine," she said. "Send it to us, and we'll publish it. Then how about coming to New York and working with us?"

(a beat)

All this within ten minutes. My head was spinning. It spun faster when the station manager asked whether I'd take over the show. Greg had already communicated his fading interest, and since my debut had gone smoothly, I was the obvious candidate. I was delighted, but worried how Greg might react. Would he be insulted? Or, worse, would he think I had stolen the job from under him? I told the manager I'd consider it.

GREG enters and sits at the table.

JULIA (CONT'D)
(to the audience)

That night I broached the issue over dinner.

(to Greg)

Did you listen to the interview with Liz Conrad?

GREG

Was that today? How'd it go?

JULIA

They told me I did a good job.

GREG

I knew it. But be careful. They flatter everybody shamelessly.

JULIA

Really.

GREG

All the time.

JULIA

Thanks. I'll keep that in mind.
(a beat)
They also said . . . they'd like me to do the show more often.

GREG

What do you mean?

JULIA

They want me to... take over... permanently.

GREG

Instead of me?

JULIA

Uh-huh.

JULIA (CONT'D)
(to the audience)
If he had become upset, I would've understood, but...
GREG
Great!
JULIA
You don't mind?
GREG
Not at all! I don't have patience for it any more. And you do. So you'll do a better job. Besides, you look stunning.

GREG leaves. SHE stands.

JULIA
(to the audience)
I didn't remind him that the show was on radio. I also didn't bring up my off-the-air conversation with Liz and the possibility I might leave Blanton. Did I feel guilty about my oversight? Of course. Did I live with it? All too easily.
(a beat)
Meanwhile Greg received a gift of his own: an invitation to present a series of lectures across the state. These cut into what would have been his writing time, but he didn't seem to care. For the first time since I had known him, he appeared both energized and at peace. He cut his drinking to an occasional cocktail, and even skipped some nights at the Eastcheap. Plus after every performance he came back glowing in triumph.

GREG enters and whirls her around a few times.

GREG
They gave me a standing ovation!
JULIA
And I'm sure you deserved it, but I'm getting dizzy!

HE stops, then holds her face.

GREG
God, you're beautiful.
JULIA
Thank you.
GREG
Have I told you that?
JULIA
Yes.
GREG
Do you mind if I say so again from time to time?

JULIA

Not at all.

GREG

You know the best thing about giving all these talks? Coming home to you.

He kisses her.

You do know that, don't you?

JULIA

I'm getting the idea.

GREG

So what are we going to do about it?

JULIA

Well...

GREG

I'll tell you. We're going to make love until my class tomorrow.

JULIA
(to the audience)

I won't burden you with details, but we came close.

GREG

I've never been so happy. And there's only one reason: you.

HE leaves.

JULIA
(to the audience)

At this confession, most women would have been delighted. I, however, wriggled uncomfortably, because I knew that our time together was grimly finite.

(a beat)

As my thesis drew to a close, Greg reviewed every word. I still didn't tell him that I had a publisher and a job waiting in the wings. You could call that a lie. It was certainly deceptive. But I had my rationale. He was still susceptible to his destructive habits: not only at the Eastcheap, but alone at home. I was the stabilizing presence in his world, the one person both necessary and sufficient for his happiness. I didn't know how long I could bear that responsibility.

(a beat)

At last my thesis was approved, and in October I became entitled to put the initials "MA" after my name. Greg and I celebrated with a delicious weekend in the mountains.

(a beat)

A day later I called Liz Conrad in New York, and she asked for the manuscript. Within a week she called back to say that she loved it. Then she surprised me: "Why not come to the city and stop by our office? You can meet everybody, and they can meet you."

JULIA (CONT'D)
(a beat)

Had Greg been in town, making the trip without his knowledge would have been impossible. But he was on one of his own excursions, so the next morning I made the journey to Manhattan. As I rode in, then bounced along the streets, I knew immediately that here was where I had to be.
(a beat)

Over lunch, Liz asked whether I was still doing the radio show. I said I was. "Perfect," she said. "We can always use someone with media experience." Then came the key question: "Are you ready to join us?"
(a beat)

"Absolutely."

GREG enters and sits at the table.

JULIA (CONT'D)
(to the audience)

Two nights later, I made Greg dinner. The whole time we were eating, I let him exult in his latest triumph. Finally, fortified by a few drinks, I set the situation in front of him.

SHE sits near him.

GREG

What kind of job are they talking about?

JULIA

Editing. Promotion. Writing more books. Giving speeches. Liz has always promised that I could branch out.

Short pause.

GREG

What do you mean "always promised"? How long have you known this woman?

JULIA

I interviewed her. Remember that first show you didn't want to do?

GREG

Yeah, I remember. And she called just now? Out of the blue?

JULIA

Well... we've been in touch. On and off.

GREG

Why didn't you say anything?

JULIA

What was there to say?

GREG

That you had possibilities. Why didn't you tell me?

JULIA

I'm telling you now! Besides, it doesn't matter when anything happened! I have an offer, and I have to decide whether to take it!

GREG

You're avoiding the question! Why didn't you tell me?

JULIA

I just got the offer yesterday!

GREG

That's not what I mean!

JULIA

Look, could we argue about this another time? I have to make a decision.
(short pause)

GREG

You mean you'd leave?

JULIA

I'm considering it.

Short pause.

GREG

What about us?

JULIA

That's... up in the air.

GREG

What does that mean? Julia, my life is here.

JULIA

Can't you find a life somewhere else?

Short pause.

GREG

You must know what I've been thinking.

JULIA

What?

GREG

That we're going to get married. And have a family.

JULIA

You never said anything!

GREG

Of course I did! You just didn't want to listen!

A beat.

JULIA

Look, you're making all this much harder! The problem is right now! Don't you get it? There's not enough to keep me here!

Pause.

GREG

Not enough to keep you here.

JULIA

I didn't mean it that way

GREG

But that's the way you said it. "There's not enough to keep me–"

JULIA

I'm sorry, okay? I didn't mean it–

GREG

In other words, I'm not enough–

JULIA

Stop it!

(short pause)

Look, what do you want?

GREG

What do *I* want?

JULIA

Yes, what do you want?

GREG

What do I want?

A beat.

JULIA

Do you want to come with me? Is that it?

GREG

You had a tough time spitting that out, didn't you?

JULIA

Do you?

GREG

Do I want to come with you?

JULIA

Well?

GREG

You certainly make the possibility enticing.

JULIA

Do you?

GREG

Let me get this straight. You're asking whether I want to surrender a tenured professorship to move to New York, where I don't know a soul and have no prospects for a job, so I can watch you gallivant around.

A beat.

JULIA

Can't you look for something?

GREG

It doesn't work that way.

JULIA

It did for me!

GREG

That's fine. Now what about me?

JULIA

You have to try!

GREG

I can't!

JULIA

Why not?

GREG

Because here is where I function! For better or worse, here is where I help people like you!

JULIA

I know! And I have thanked you, again and again.

GREG

And now you're finished with me.

JULIA

I never said that! But I have an incredible opportunity. Which you seem determined to block!

GREG

And which you are going to take. No matter how I feel about it.

Short pause.

JULIA

I invited you to come with me.

GREG

Only after I dragged it out of you.

Short pause.

JULIA

Look, I know this is all sudden.

GREG

No, it isn't! You've been mulling it over for what... a year?

JULIA

Well...

GREG

You could've mentioned it before. Then we could've talked about it.

JULIA

There wasn't anything definite!

GREG

Were you afraid I might say yes?

JULIA

Of course not!

GREG

Maybe you figure I'll hold you back.

JULIA

I never said that!

GREG

Then let's make it official: do you... want me... to join you in New York?

Pause.

JULIA

Yes.

GREG laughs quietly.

GREG

Talk about a heartfelt entreaty.

JULIA

I said yes!

GREG

And you so obviously meant it.

JULIA

Look, no matter how I said it, I asked. And you said no. Now what do you expect me to do? I'm grateful to you. I am very grateful. But I don't think I owe you the rest of my life!

Pause.

GREG

I'm sorry. I don't want to give you problems, but I'm little taken aback by everything that's come out tonight. Can you understand that?

JULIA

Yes.

GREG

Well, at least we agree on something.
> *(a beat)*

Do me one favor.

JULIA

What?

GREG

While you're working all this out, remember one thing: jobs come and go. But what you and I have had is forever.

> *HE leaves.*

JULIA
> *(to the audience)*

For the rest of the night, questions raced through my mind. Did Greg love me as much as he claimed? Or did he just want me around to brace his ego? I even considered whether he was afraid I'd end up more successful than he.

> *(a beat)*

I reminded myself how much he had done for me. Did he believe that I owed him? *Did I owe him?*

> *(a beat)*

If I left, his world might collapse. He'd start drinking and… I didn't want to imagine any more.

> *(a beat)*

Then I reached the hardest question: how did I feel about Greg? He was brilliant and entertaining, and we had enjoyed marvelous times. But was I ready share my life with him?

> *(a beat)*

By morning the truth hit. Greg felt just the way he said: he loved me. And I loved… being with him on the Blanton campus. Which would always be his home.

> *(a beat)*

I was on my way to New York. My new home. Where I didn't want him to absorb my time, my energy, and my attention.

> *(a beat)*

I wanted to devote it all to… me.

> *(a beat)*

Virginia Woolf famously wrote that for a woman to write fiction, she needs a room of her own. I wanted the whole house.

> *(a beat)*

I dreaded telling him what I had decided, so for a couple of days I kept out of sight. He didn't call. We finally saw each other outside the Department.

> *GREG enters.*

GREG

Hi.

JULIA

Hi.

GREG

Missed you lately.

JULIA

Me, too. I guess we've just...

GREG

Missed each other.

(short pause)

Any news?

JULIA

I think so.

GREG

And?

JULIA

I have to give it a try.

GREG

And by "it," I presume you mean the New York job.

JULIA

Right.

Short pause.

GREG

Sure you're doing the right thing?

JULIA

No.

GREG

But you have to try.

JULIA

I think so.

GREG

If it matters, I agree.

HE pats her shoulder.

See ya'.

JULIA
(to the audience)

That afternoon I resigned my spring teaching slot, and during the next month and a half I gradually relocated to Manhattan. Meanwhile Greg remained amiable.

GREG

Need help packing?

JULIA

Everything's under control.

GREG

Good, good. But if problems come up, I'm here for you.

JULIA

I know.

GREG

You can always count on me, right?

JULIA

Right.

GREG leaves.

JULIA (CONT'D)
(to the audience)

At moments like that, I almost second-guessed myself. Was I making the right decision? How can we ever know?
(a beat)
The night before I left, I stopped at his house. The minute I saw him, I knew that he had been drinking. A lot. He was unshaven and probably hadn't changed clothes for days.

GREG enters and sits.

JULIA (CONT'D)
(to the audience)

I tried to be upbeat.
(to Greg)
Keep up your writing. I can't wait to read that history of American drama.

GREG

Don't hold your breath.

JULIA

You'll make it.
(pause)
Well, I have to get going. Early start tomorrow.
(a beat)
I don't mind telling you. I'm a little scared.

GREG

Don't be ridiculous. You'll knock 'em out.

A beat.

JULIA

I'll keep in touch.

GREG

Please do.

JULIA

And I'm sure I'll visit soon.

GREG

I'll look forward to that.

(a beat)

Have a good trip.

JULIA

Thanks. And thanks again for everything. Without you, none of this would ever have happened–

GREG

Right, right.

HE leaves. Pause.

JULIA

(to the audience)

As I left, part of me was heartbroken. But I left.

(a beat)

After I settled in Manhattan, my circle of acquaintances grew exponentially: first the women in the office, then a stream of writers, editors, agents, and publishers. Yet Greg was never far from my mind. Every time I reviewed someone's work and suggested refining structure, language, or logic, I heard his voice. Every time I spoke in public, I heard his phrases. Every time I attended a play or concert, I wondered how he'd comment about it.

(a beat)

At night, in my apartment, I missed his stories. And his arms around me.

(a beat)

When my book was published, I dedicated it this way: "To Greg, who made this book possible." I sent him a copy, as well as flyers about upcoming talks and clippings from appearances. He never replied. When I called, he was rarely home, and when we did speak, his answers were perfunctory. I began to lose touch.

(a beat)

Sometimes, though, life leads us where we have no intention of going.

JULIA (CONT'D)
(a beat)

Two years after I joined the firm, Liz asked me to visit a high school near Blanton, and I couldn't help swinging by my old haunt. The day before, I'd left a message on Greg's phone, telling him when I'd drop by.
(a beat)

The lawn was un-mowed. The house seemed rundown, almost ramshackle. I rang the bell.

GREG enters and sits.

GREG

Yeah!

JULIA
(to the audience)

The smell suggested that the area hadn't been cleaned in months. He was in his study, plopped in his chair, surrounded by papers.

GREG

Hiya.

JULIA
(to the audience)

He had aged ten years.

GREG

How ya' doin'?

JULIA
(to Greg)

Fine.

GREG

Workin' hard?

JULIA

You know how it is.

GREG

No, I don't. That's why I asked.

JULIA laughs lightly.

JULIA

How're your classes?

GREG

I try to show up.

JULIA

I assume they're still fun.

GREG

As stimulating as ever. In fact, I can't wait to wake up every morning. That's why I usually don't bother going to sleep at night.

JULIA

I presume your students still idolize you.

GREG

I don't know what they think.

Pause.

JULIA

How's your book coming?

GREG

What book? Oh, yeah. My book. My tome. You know, I've been so busy that I haven't been able to work on it. I really ought to start again.

(pause)

JULIA

Well, I don't want to take any more of your time. And I have to be in the city tomorrow.

GREG

Of course you do. Amazing they can run the place without you.

JULIA

I'll try to come back soon.

GREG

I can't wait. Forgive me for not getting up, but this essay is fascinating, and I don't want to lose momentum.

Pause. HE stumbles to his feet, then leaves slowly.

JULIA
(to the audience)

On the trip back, I told myself that I was not responsible for what had happened to him, that we all have to stand on our own. From that moment on, I never tried to contact him. I never sent him anything. I tried to stop thinking about him, and I am not proud to report that I was largely successful.

(a beat)

Over the following years, I enjoyed working at the office, but I was also determined to find a wider stage. Since I had no family responsibilities, I accepted all long-distance opportunities to spread the company's message at schools, colleges, and professional conferences, and on television and radio. I relished it all. I heard myself praised as a shrewd critic of literature and an inspiration to creative women. All palaver, of course, but intoxicating palaver.

JULIA (CONT'D)
(a beat, to the audience)

People thought *I* was impressive. Ten minutes listening to Greg blast out ideas would have left them overwhelmed.

(a beat)

I reminded myself that I owed him a visit. Yet the opportunity never arose. Maybe I didn't look hard enough.

(a beat)

In case you're interested. I met plenty of men. Most were probably grateful that I never exerted pressure for commitment. Yet I like to believe that a few regretted how I wasn't more receptive to their intimations about a permanent relationship.

(a beat)

Sometimes I recalled the words of Marie Corelli: "I never married," she wrote, "because I have three pets at home that answer the same purpose as a husband. I have a dog that growls, a parrot that swears all afternoon, and a cat that comes home late at night."

(a beat)

Finally, during one of my spring tours, I was booked to speak at Blanton. In contrast to New York, the place looked... I'm sorry, but the word is "piddling." Afterwards, the new Department Assistant handed me a note from Greg inviting me to his home. When she asked if I had his address out of town, I panicked. Had he fallen so far that he had lost his house? I was terrified at what I might find, then relieved that the location was in the new complex he and I had passed years before.

(a beat)

I was surprised that the garage held two cars. When I rang the bell, a woman in her thirties answered. She smiled graciously, identified herself as Laura, and led me into the immaculate living room, where Greg sat reading on a modular sofa. His eyes were bright, and his hair was thin, but trimmed.

GREG enters.

GREG
You made it!

HE hugs her.

JULIA
You look great!

GREG
A little older and a little thicker, but feeling good, thanks to you know who.

JULIA
(to the audience)

He put his arm around Laura. I wondered how much he had told her about me. Then I realized that it didn't matter.

GREG

And if you look out this window, you'll see our daughter.
(calling)
Heather, would you come here please?

JULIA

(to the audience)

A girl of five or so was playing on a swing set, but at the sound of Greg's voice she ran to his arms. Yes, she was adorable. Most of her features were Laura's, but her brown eyes were Greg's.
(a beat)
Laura took Heather outside so Greg and I could talk. As they left, Greg gazed after them more lovingly than he ever had looked at me.

GREG

I see your name all the time. You're almost famous, aren't you?

JULIA

I suppose. What about your book? Did you ever finish it?

GREG

Never came close. In fact, I dropped the project years ago.

JULIA

Working on any else?

GREG

Not really. I don't have the drive any more. Besides, Laura's helped me realize that teaching's what I do best, so why shouldn't I enjoy it? You'll also be glad to know that I haven't had a drink in years. Think there might be a connection?
(a beat)
I guess I've found that other things are more important. What about you? Met anybody?

JULIA

It's tough when I'm always on the move.

GREG

Don't worry. Somebody wonderful is right around the corner. And when he finds you, he'll be a lucky guy.

JULIA

(to the audience)

Did I hear a mocking inflection in his voice? Then he brought me up to date about a few campus characters. But I could barely listen, because the more he talked, the more mundane his life seemed. I tried to tell him about people I'd met and places I'd been, but he just smiled vaguely. Before long, uncomfortable pauses intruded, and in less than an hour I was desperate to leave.

              JULIA (CONT'D)
              (to Greg)
I'm glad to see you so happy.
                GREG
Couldn't be better. You're staying for dinner, aren't you?
                JULIA
I'd love to, but I have to hurry back.
                GREG
The classic words of a classic go-getter.
              (a beat)
I'm very proud of you. I hope you know that.
                JULIA
I owe everything to you.
                GREG
Glad I could help.
              HE kisses her cheek and leaves.
                JULIA
              (to the audience)
He called Laura and Heather, and we all said good-bye. After I closed the door, I glanced through the window and saw Heather nestled in his lap.
              (a beat)
During the trip to Manhattan, I considered how far I'd moved beyond Greg. But I also couldn't forget that last glimpse of Heather, and by the time I reached Penn Station, I realized that, in his own way, Greg had moved beyond me.
              (a beat)
I cut down on my traveling. Running around the country no longer had appeal.
              (a beat)
I had another reason: Charles McCallister. He was Chairman of a foundation that helped support Womanbooks, and a lot of my friends told me that he was worth the effort. So when he pursued, I didn't resist. I watched performances at the Metropolitan Opera from eighth row, center aisle, as well as games at Yankee Stadium from his box. We also shared two vacations in his home in the Bahamas. I attended gatherings at his Fifth Avenue duplex, where I met eminent figures in the corporate and artistic communities. Thanks to those connections, I became a consultant here and an advisor someplace else. My income swelled.
              (a beat)
He was also a gentleman in every sense of the word. No surprise, then, that everyone assumed we would marry. One night, Charles put it on the line: he wanted a partner for life. How could any woman say no?

JULIA (CONT'D)
(short pause)
I did.
(a beat)
Possibly I had never learned the theme of *The Taming of the Shrew*: that the greatest joy comes from giving of oneself. Before long, though, the real answer became apparent. Charles was generous, well-bred, and rich. I, however, wanted someone tempestuous, earthy, brooding, and brilliant. In other words, I wanted one particular man who was utterly wrong for me. But he was still the only man I would ever want.
(short pause)
To ease my pain, I moved from the studio apartment I had occupied since coming to New York into a six-room spectacular on Riverside Drive, with a panoramic view of the Hudson. I decorated it just as I wanted, and gave lots of parties and met lots of people. How many? Name three of today's most famous writers, and I guarantee that at least two of them have dined at my table.
(a beat)
But whenever the last celebrant departed, I found myself alone. That's when I thought of Greg. Sometimes I imagined us trading byplay as we undressed, then embraced out of the sheer bliss of being with each other.
(a beat)
Meanwhile my base of operations remained the office, where one day a young woman interviewed for an internship. She had just received her BA from Blanton, so I made sure to meet her. She told me that Greg had retired because of ill health. Apparently all those hard years had finally taken their toll. I resolved to go see him, but I couldn't find time.
(short pause)
Fifteen months later, I received a phone call from Laura. Greg had died.
(short pause)
During the funeral I stood next to her and Heather to offer consolation. Both held up well. So did I through most of it, but when they lowered the... into the ground, I started to quiver. Heather took my arm. She's blossomed into a lovely young woman. Greg must have been a wonderful father.
(a beat)
Since his death, one idea keeps recurring to me. Greg always insisted that to succeed, writers have to be selfish. He liked to believe that he had that quality. He didn't. But I did. He had ambitions, but I was the one who carried them out. Everything he wanted to be? That's what I became. And all because of what he–
The next words catch in her throat. SHE gathers herself.
How about Greg himself? For so long he wanted what he couldn't have: a sterling reputation as a writer and thinker.

JULIA (CONT'D)
And what he did have, the capacity to inspire others, he dismissed. Thank goodness for Laura. She helped him appreciate his own gifts. Could I have done as much?

(a beat)

Had I stayed, I might have spared him rough times. He might even have finished that book. And a few more. But what about me?

(a beat)

Should I apologize for enjoying what I've done? Had I married Greg, I wouldn't have accomplished ten per cent of it. Of course, I would've had other things...

(short pause)

We all make choices, and our choices have consequences. I'll always have regrets. But then... who doesn't?

(short pause)

One more tidbit to share with you. At the funeral Laura gave me a letter. She found it in Greg's desk, addressed to me, but never sent. It's dated many years ago, right after I returned to Blanton that first time after leaving.

GREG enters.

JULIA (CONT'D)
(to the audience)

Dearest Julia...

GREG (SIMULTANEOUSLY WITH JULIA)
Dearest Julia...

JULIA stops.

GREG (CONT'D)
(to the audience)

I hope this missive finds you well. I myself am a disaster area, but that doesn't matter. What does is how pleased I am for you. My great regret is that I cannot share your success. Because I know your mind and heart, I fear you believe that your extraordinary ascent and my precipitous decline are connected. Please dismiss such considerations. My misfortunes are my responsibility, and I wish you only good things. Love, Greg.

HE leaves.

JULIA
(to the audience)

When I first read those words, I told myself that he was letting me off the hook. Then I remembered that the letter had not been mailed. Maybe he never did forgive me.

SHE begins to gather her papers.

Oh, yes. Earlier I mentioned some astonishing news. It came this morning. And after all I've explained it, you'll understand why it unsettled me.

JULIA (CONT'D)
(a beat)

When Greg passed away, the University honored him by creating an award in his name for an alum who has become distinguished in the arts. In a couple of weeks I'm headed to Blanton for the presentation of the first winner. Would you care to guess that person's name?

SHE raises her hand.

The irony does not escape me.
(a beat)

The ceremony will include tributes to Greg, and various speakers are sure to tell stories about his magic in the classroom and his devotion to his students. I'll pretend to listen, but I'll be remembering him in my own way: private moments, some joyous, some not, but almost certainly the most important of my life.
(a beat)

Finally they'll introduce the guest of honor. I'll be expected to mention all the people who have influenced me, but I really have only one person to thank. And he won't be there.
(pause)

I'm aware that you came here expecting me to speak about women and writing. But rest assured that I've covered a lot of the same material, just from a different perspective. I had no intention of becoming so intimate, but sometimes these things take on a life of their own.
(a beat)

So... thank you very much. Goodnight.

CURTAIN.

A Farce Noir by
Victor L. Cahn

www.stagerights.com

PRODUCTION HISTORY

SHEEPSKIN was originally a one-act play produced by Prism Theater (Ron Comenzo and Stephen-Stewart James, Artistic Producers) at the Perry Street Theater, New York, NY, February 1-28, 1982. The cast included Ed Setrakian, Rochelle Owens, and Patricia Kalember. The Director was Victor Argo.

A two-act version was produced at Caffé Lena Theater, Saratoga Springs, NY, March 8-10, 1992. The cast included Victor L. Cahn and Carol Max. The Director was Joan Pendergast.

SUMMARY

A male professor of English tries to manipulate a female graduate student for his own amusement, but she proves more resourceful than he anticipated.

CHARACTERS

WYATT: 50-55, a professor of English
SHARON: 30-35, a graduate student in English

SCENE

The Place: The living room of Wyatt's house, near the campus of a university.
The Time: Not very long ago.

ACT I:

Scene 1: A late afternoon in September.

Scene 2: A week later. Evening.

ACT II:

Scene 1: Three evenings later.

Scene 2: Three weeks later. Evening

Scene 3: A week later. Evening.

Scene 4: Five weeks later. Evening.

SETTING

The living room is filled with a hodgepodge of furniture. In the CENTER is a sofa, next to it a large, overstuffed chair with a hassock in front. Nearby is a desk piled high with papers and binders. UPSTAGE is a small bar. OFFSTAGE is the bedroom. TO THE SIDE a bookcase overflows with books and journals.

ACT ONE

SCENE ONE

A LATE AFTERNOON IN SEPTEMBER.

PROFESSOR WYATT RANDALL sits in the chair, his feet on the hassock. HE reads a magazine. The doorbell rings. HE tosses the magazine to the floor.

WYATT
Coming!

HE opens the door to find SHARON SANDERS, wearing running clothes and carrying a binder thick with paper. SHE is disheveled and slightly out of breath.

SHARON
Professor Randall?

WYATT
Is it Miss Sanders?

SHARON
Sharon Sanders. Hi!

SHE offers her hand. HE shakes it.

WYATT
How do you do?

SHARON
Just fine, thank you!

WYATT
Come on in.

SHE enters, and HE closes the door

SHARON
Thanks! I hope I'm not too early–

WYATT
Not at all–

SHARON
... 'cause I tried to time my jog over from the Quad.

WYATT
You ran all the way?

SHARON
I run every afternoon!

WYATT

Really–

SHARON

So I decided to kill two birds. But I never run with a watch. I figure all that bouncing'll damage the spring or something. I don't know. So I may be a little early. Hope it's no trouble.

WYATT

To the contrary. It's been a dull afternoon–

SHARON

Great!

(a beat)

Oh! Not that it's great your afternoon was dull. Just that I'm glad I'm not interrupting anything... unless I am– well, you know what I mean.

WYATT

Of course.

(pointing to the sofa)

Please.

SHARON

Thanks!

> *SHE sits on the sofa. HE sits in the chair opposite her.*

SHARON (CONT'D)

I know I'm a mess–

WYATT

Not at all–

SHARON

No, I am, I am! But after three miles... I just hope you don't have to fumigate. Am I sweating too much? I probably shouldn't have shown up this way. But some habits are hard to break, right? Anyway, I'm out there every day, trudging along. Not fast, but steady. And I've been doing it for so long, and... well, habits are hard to break. I said that already, didn't I? Am I talking too much? I'm sorry. I always do that when I'm... you know–

WYATT

You're doing fine–

SHARON

You're sure?

WYATT

I wouldn't say it if I–

SHARON

Of course not! I'm sorry!

WYATT
But if I may get in a word…
SHARON
Go ahead, please!
WYATT
I admire anyone who shows such discipline.
SHARON
Oh, boy! I never know how to handle compliments like that. I just babble. Although that's what I've been doing anyway, right? When I'm nervous, that's what I do. I babble. I can't help it. I just babble. Although sometimes I head over to the gym.
WYATT
Between babbles?
SHARON
Instead of running.
(realizing that He made a joke)
Oh!

SHE laughs.

WYATT
And what happens there?
SHARON
You won't believe it. I row. In the tanks. Where the crew works out.

SHE mimes rowing.

Strange, right? How many women strokers do you know?
(a beat)
WYATT
I couldn't say.
SHARON
Most people think it's bizarre, but I don't mind. I started back in prep school. We all had to do something athletic, and at camp I used to like to paddle canoes. So before I knew it, there I was, like Huckleberry Finn, living on the river. I did it the last two years of high school and the first year of college. Used to get out at six o'clock in the morning, then go back in the afternoon. It was crazy, but I loved it. Did you ever row?

WYATT shakes his head.

SHARON (CONT'D)
Then you must think I'm nuts, too. Everybody says the same thing. What kind of sport is it where you win sitting on your butt moving backwards? Right?

WYATT
Well—

SHARON
But you just cannot appreciate the feeling that surges through your body! The energy— it's incredible! Even though I was always last substitute on the last boat.

WYATT
Why'd you give it up? Too much time?

SHARON
That. And you should have seen those girls who did it much longer.

SHE holds her hands wide apart.

No way I was going to have shoulders bigger than the guys I was going with. So now I do it just for fun. What about you? Did you ever play anything?

WYATT
I used to be a whiz at quoits.

SHARON
Quoits! You're kidding!
(a beat)
Of course you are! How could I even ask such a question? You must think I am an absolute idiot—

WYATT
Ms. Sanders—

SHARON
But I guess between my running and my rowing, and my complete state of panic over this, I'm a wreck.

SHE waves the binder.

I mean, the last few months have been crazy—

WYATT
Sharon, if I may—

SHARON
Hmmm?

WYATT
Calm down.

SHARON
Okay.

SHE takes a deep breath.

All I wanted to say was that—

WYATT
No, no. Get a hold of yourself. Then tell me—
SHARON
I'm fine. Really, I am—
WYATT
I'm sure you are. But take a minute.
SHARON
Okay, but—
WYATT
And don't say a word.
SHARON
I just wanted to tell you that I—
WYATT
(raising an open palm)
It'll hold.

> *SHARON mouths "Okay" and waves her own hand to proclaim silence. SHE takes a huge breath and leans back.*
>
> *Pause.*

WYATT (CONT'D)
First, in response to your questions, no, I don't row. I don't run. I don't play tennis or golf. In fact, I don't play anything.
SHARON
Not even a little? Just to get the ol' heart pumping?

> *HE holds up a cautionary finger.*

Sorry. Calming down.
WYATT
I have always followed the advice of a former colleague, now eighty-seven and in the best of health: "I get all the exercise I need attending the funerals of my friends who exercise."
SHARON
Now you're being silly.

> *SHE looks aghast. HE smiles.*

SHARON (CONT'D)
Tell me I didn't say that.
WYATT
Quite all right. Even so, I suspect we'd better move ahead in our discussion—

SHARON

Good idea!

WYATT

—to that thick binder you're clutching so firmly against your chest.

SHARON

Right! Here!

SHE gives him the binder

SHARON (CONT'D)

And I want to thank you for being one of my readers.

WYATT

Not at all. Happy to help. When George Buhl asked me to join the team, he said only positive things about you: smart, hard-working, scholarly…

SHARON

Wow! I hope I can live up to all that!

WYATT

I'm sure you will.

SHARON

Even so, I appreciate your giving up your time.

WYATT

Don't worry about it. I can't speak for anybody else, but for me, reading a first-rate doctoral dissertation remains one of the pleasures of our profession.

SHARON

That's good to know! And I think it's ready. At least, I hope so! I mean, after all those months in the library, and tons of reading… sometimes I look back, and I can't believe what I've managed to do in three years!

WYATT

It's a great feeling, isn't it? To know that you've made the effort, and that you have something worthwhile to show for it, something to be proud of.

SHARON

That's it exactly.

WYATT

Hey, we've all been there! By the way, thanks for agreeing to stop here today. I hope it wasn't too inconvenient.

SHARON

Oh, no problem! As I said, I run anyway—

WYATT

The thing is, I didn't have any meetings or classes scheduled, and I always try to avoid unnecessary visits to the Department. That's one way to stay out of trouble. Although those interoffice envelopes still show up.

WYATT (CONT'D)

I always wonder, is anything more depressing than an interoffice envelope? In twenty-three years, I don't think I've ever received one that contained good news.

SHARON

I know what you mean.

WYATT

'Nuff said. Let's not ruin a pleasant occasion. Now, if you don't mind, let me find out where we stand.

SHARON

Terrific!

WYATT

I assume you've fulfilled all the other requirements for the degree.

SHARON

Every one.

WYATT

Language exam?

SHARON

Four years ago.

WYATT

Comprehensive exams?

SHARON

Two years ago.

WYATT

Then this is it. Once the dissertation is approved, and you pass the defense, you are transformed into Dr. Sanders, Ph.D., empowered to spread knowledge and goodness through the groves of academe.

SHARON

I can't believe it'll ever happen. After all these years…

WYATT

You can't wait to start teaching.

SHARON

Right.

WYATT

Well, I'll do everything I can for you.

SHARON

That makes me feel a lot better.

WYATT

Good. I assume you've completed all your courses.

SHARON
Every lous– uh, every single one.
(a beat)
Not that I didn't enjoy them. And I learned a lot.
WYATT
But they still took plenty of time.
SHARON
They really did. Is that a terrible thing to say?
WYATT
Not to me. As I said, I went through it all myself. A long time ago.
SHARON
Not so long, I'll bet.
WYATT
You're very kind. Now let's get back to you. Your primary field is the Renaissance, right?
SHARON
Right.
WYATT
And what classes did you take in that area?
SHARON
Oh, lots. Let's see. The first was Elizabethan and Jacobean Drama.
WYATT
With Barney Palmer?
SHARON
Yup.
WYATT
That must have been fascinating.
SHARON
Kinda weird, actually. I mean, I know he's a great scholar.
WYATT
One of the best. But…
SHARON
But…
WYATT
A little past his prime?
SHARON
I'm glad you said it.

WYATT
Maybe a lot past?

SHARON
Maybe.

WYATT
What did he pull on you?

SHARON
Well, nothing on me personally…

WYATT
That was a good break.

SHARON
But he kinda overpacked the reading list.

WYATT
Typical.

SHARON
Then, with about four weeks to go, he announced that we'd never finish all the plays he'd assigned.

WYATT
Again, an old story.

SHARON
Well, everyone in the class expected him just to drop a few.

WYATT
That'd be logical.

SHARON
But instead he said, "Since we'll never finish all the readings, I'm cancelling the rest of our classes."

Short pause.

WYATT
You're kidding.

SHARON
I swear. We couldn't believe it.

WYATT
That's wild, even by Barney's standards.

SHARON
At least he gave me an A.

WYATT
I'm surprised he bothered to grade your papers.

SHARON
I'm not sure he did.

WYATT

You're probably right. Well, he has only one more year to go. Then we'll get some fresh blood in here. What else did you take?

SHARON

Renaissance poetry.

WYATT

Alice Holtzman.

SHARON

She was great.

WYATT

Good ol' Alice. She gave me one of my favorite lines about professors. She teaches only one day a week, you know. On Wednesdays.

SHARON

Can she get away with that?

WYATT

Trust me.

SHARON

Of course! I didn't mean–

WYATT

Anyway, a few years ago, when George was just starting as Director of Graduate Studies, he asked Alice to teach her one course on Monday instead of Wednesday. That way all our classes wouldn't be offered in the same half-dozen slots. Well, at this innocent request, Alice's face just dropped. "Monday?" she said. I mean, she was horrified. And George said, "Yeah. Is that all right?" To which Alice replied, "But if you don't have Mondays, what do you have?"

SHARON

That's unbelievable.

WYATT

Can you imagine if she had to work for a living?

SHARON

Oh, boy…

WYATT

My sentiments exactly.
    (a beat)
You know what?

SHARON

What?

WYATT

I've managed to depress myself. To cheer me up, tell me about the best course you ever had here.

SHARON

The best? Ooooh, that's hard.

WYATT

Try, anyway, 'cause we want to finish the evening on a positive note.

SHARON

Wait! I can tell you. My final seminar last spring.

WYATT

Which was… ?

SHARON

Prose of the Romantic Era.

WYATT

Nan Blocker!

SHARON

She was wonderful!

WYATT

Oh, Nan's a quality woman. Demands the best from herself. Demands it from her students.

SHARON

That's just how she was.

WYATT

Too bad we're going to lose her.

SHARON

No!

WYATT

Hm-mmm.

SHARON

Where's she going?

WYATT

Search me. All I know is that this is the last year of her contract. And she's not being reappointed.

SHARON

Why not?

WYATT shrugs.

SHARON (CONT'D)

There must be a reason. I mean, she's a topnotch teacher. And she's published a lot. That book on Keats. It's first-rate.

WYATT
Very impressive.
SHARON
Does she have another job?
WYATT
Not that I'm aware of. Her career would seem ingloriously terminated. At least temporarily.
SHARON
Then why is she leaving?
WYATT
No room here. She came with a three-year contract and...
SHARON
It's over?
WYATT
Sad, right? With all the dead wood piling up at this place, you'd think we could find a spot for someone as gifted as she is.
SHARON
That's so disappointing.
WYATT
Isn't it? Although I don't mind telling you that several men in the Department, along with a couple of women, are more than willing to show Ms. Blocker the door.
SHARON
Why am I not surprised?
(a beat)
Although it isn't my place to comment.
WYATT
No, no, go ahead.
SHARON
I shouldn't.
WYATT
It's okay. I'm always curious about what our students are thinking.
SHARON
Well... she might be too aggressive. Too outspoken.
WYATT
And folks tend not to embrace those qualities in a woman.
SHARON
I'm afraid so. I mean, you have to stand up for your convictions. But she should probably do it less...

WYATT

Stridently?

SHARON

You have to be subtle.

WYATT

True, true. You'll be glad to know that a few of us fought for her. But too many senior folks were adamant. No money available. Or so they said.

SHARON

You don't believe them.

WYATT

The official word is that they want to appoint all the women they can. Unofficially, I think we know the real story.

SHARON

A lot of us'll miss her.

WYATT

Tell me about it. I hate to say so, but this can be a harsh business. We like to pretend that we dwell strictly in the realm of intellect, but too often reality raises its ugly head.

HE reflects.

You and I, however, have our own priorities.

HE taps the dissertation.

I hope to start reading tonight, although, as always, work is piling up. They're at me from all sides.

SHARON

I'm sure.

WYATT

But we won't let ourselves be distracted. When would you like to get together again?

SHARON

At your convenience.

WYATT

Let's see. This week is crowded. Class tomorrow. Office hours the next day. Meeting of the Curriculum Committee the day after that.

SHARON

You name the day and time.

WYATT

Whatever I do, I'll try not to pull a Barney Palmer on you. He once kept a student's dissertation on his desk for six months without looking at it.

WYATT (CONT'D)
The student lost a job, not to mention piles of money. Then she sued the University. The whole thing turned into a mess.
SHARON
I think I'm getting nervous again.
WYATT
Don't worry. You'll be fine. But I have to tell you. Sometimes I wonder how many outstanding scholars we've lost because they couldn't survive the hoops and hurdles we set up for them.
HE ruminates.
Anyway, the question remains: when shall we two meet again?
SHARON
How about next week?
WYATT
A week from today?
SHARON
Is that too soon?
WYATT
Absolutely not. Is this time all right?
SHARON
Well...
WYATT
Or do you usually work out now? No need to interfere with the rest of your life.
SHARON
No, no! I don't want anything to get in our way.
WYATT
But I want to be flexible. How about seven?
SHARON
In your office?
WYATT
Or here. Unless this is inconvenient.
HE stands and moves to the door. SHE follows.
WYATT (CONT'D)
As one of my old instructors used to say, meeting off-campus removes the curse of formality.
SHARON
I guess this is fine.

WYATT

Then it's settled. Seven o'clock. One week from tonight. And we'll try to move you right along.

HE opens the door.

SHARON

Wonderful.

WYATT

Row, row your boat.

SHE leaves.

SHARON
(laughing)

Bye-bye. And thanks.

WYATT

My pleasure. So long.

HE closes the door. HE returns to his chair and picks up the dissertation. HE skims, then turns to the end. HE tosses the dissertation aside, then retrieves his magazine and resumes reading it.

END OF SCENE ONE

SCENE TWO

A WEEK LATER. EVENING.

WYATT is in his chair, reading. The doorbell rings. HE goes to the door.

WYATT

On my way!

HE opens the door. SHARON enters, wearing slacks and a sweater, and carrying a handbag.

SHARON

Hi, there!

WYATT

C'mon in! Good to see you.

As SHE enters, HE closes the door behind her.

And how was today's workout?

SHARON

Oh, I ran my couple of miles.

WYATT

And did you hit the oars?

SHARON

'Fraid not. Didn't feel like it.

WYATT

Nothing wrong, I trust.

HE points to the sofa.

SHARON
(sitting)

No, no. I just have to be in the right mood.
(a beat)
Maybe I was nervous about tonight.

WYATT

Even so, your dedication overwhelms me.

HE sits in his chair.

In fact, I was so inspired I tried a little exercise myself.

SHARON

Good for you!

WYATT

Walked all the way from one side of my office to the other.

SHARON
(laughing)

I should have figured as much.

WYATT
Then I went over to the gym.
SHARON
And?
WYATT
Drove right past it.
SHARON
You're incorrigible.

WYATT stands and walks to his desk.

SHARON (CONT'D)
I meant to tell you the other night. This is such a comfy place.
WYATT
The remnants of an ill-fated marriage.
SHARON
Oh! I'm sorry.
WYATT
Ancient history.

HE searches through binders and papers.

SHARON
It's the first professor's home I've seen here.
WYATT
Is that so? Too bad. We really ought to get together... I mean, faculty and students... we ought to meet more often. What did one of my instructors tell me? Remove the curse of formality.
(a beat)
But enough small talk. I finished reading your dissertation last night. Now all I have to do is find it.

HE searches through a pile of material. HE picks up a thick binder.

SHARON
I don't think that's it–
WYATT
No, no, no! This isn't yours. For which you can be enormously grateful.
SHARON
Why's that?
WYATT
Are you sure you want to hear?
SHARON
I don't know...

WYATT
I don't think you do.
(a beat)
On the other hand... you're entitled to a bit of amusement. Right?

SHARON
Whatever you–

WYATT
You know how badly these things are usually written. Awkward, stuffy, no style or grace. Well, this one plunges to new depths. 300 pages of mush!
HE flips through.
Like this: "And thus the consciousness achieved by Roderick, so endemic to his personality, and yet at the same time antithetical to the background and culture from which he has emerged, seems as yet on the whole buttressed by values which he himself attempts to strip himself thereof and thus culminates in the crisis, one might say, even the climax, of James's thesis."
(a beat)
Can you believe that?

SHARON
That's awful! I mean, I don't have the right to judge–

WYATT
Of course it's awful! And you certainly do have the right! You recognize junk when you hear it.
HE tosses the binder to the floor.
But we don't want to become unduly depressed. Shall we get to yours?
HE walks around his chair.
It has to be here. I remember reading it.

SHARON
SHE laughs lightly.
Is that good?

WYATT
Well... we'll certainly see, won't we?
HE pulls out a binder from underneath.
Ah!

SHARON
That's it.

WYATT
Your magnum opus.
HE settles in his chair.
Are we ready?

SHARON

Ready.

WYATT

Good! Now! First of all...

HE opens the binder.

First of all...

HE flips through some pages.

First of all... let me say... right off... that I enjoyed reading this very much.

SHARON

Really?

WYATT

As we've noted, these dissertations are usually so badly written... well, I don't have to go further. You know what they sound like.

SHARON

You just gave me an example–

WYATT

But yours is graceful indeed. It has a lilt, a charm, a panache. I might even say that your personality comes through in your writing. And that's about the highest compliment I can pay.

SHARON

Thank you!

WYATT

And I can see as well all the work that's gone into this project.

SHARON

Two whole years of writing. Plus a lot more, if you count research and everything else–

WYATT

Though, naturally, the amount of time really doesn't matter–

SHARON

I thought you wanted to know–

WYATT

Does it?

Short pause.

SHARON

I guess not.

WYATT

You're right. It doesn't matter. Because as impressed as I am with your effort... I do have a few reservations.

SHARON

I have to expect that.

WYATT

Indeed. It comes with the territory. But let's not hurry. Let's start from the beginning and see what we can do to help you along. Okay?

SHARON

Okay.

WYATT

Okay.

(a beat)

For instance, your title: "Matriarchal Images in the Elizabethan Renaissance: A Study of Shakespeare's Women." Now that's a fascinating topic–

SHARON

I really enjoyed working on it. Now that the field is expanding so fast–

WYATT

Just a minute–

SHARON

But my approach is unusual, in that it brings–

WYATT

The problem is that a few things–

SHARON

–together new criticism that to this point–

WYATT

Let's wait until–

SHARON

I only wanted to say–

WYATT

Let me speak for a minute, please?

HE smiles.

I'd like to point out a couple of things. If you don't mind.

SHARON

I'm sorry. I didn't mean to–

WYATT

Thank you. Certainly women characters are a fertile field.

HE laughs.

Pardon the metaphor. Ill chosen. At any rate, it's a very important subject. But, as I say, I have reservations.

SHARON
I realize that, but–
WYATT
Don't rush me. Please.
(a beat)
Preparation of the dissertation takes time, if you're going to do it properly. Try to be patient.
SHARON
I am trying–
WYATT
Try harder.

Short pause.

SHARON
I'm sure you understand my anxiety.
WYATT
Of course–
SHARON
It's a tough time–
WYATT
A very tough time. There's tremendous responsibility, pressure. You feel a compulsion to get on with it. Am I right?
SHARON
To an extent–
WYATT
Then I'm right.

HE smiles. SHARON nods. A beat.

WYATT (CONT'D)
But I certainly hope you won't allow this pressure to sway you from the ideals I know you support.
SHARON
I'll try not to. But I have a good deal at stake.
WYATT
I know. You could even say we're playing for keeps. Then again, there are many roads to success, not only along the paths of academe, but in countless fields of endeavor–
SHARON
Couldn't we stick to the topic?
WYATT
Of course.

WYATT (CONT'D)
(a beat)

Ah, the mind. The human mind. With all its vicissitudes and vagaries, its myriad meanderings—

SHARON

Please.

WYATT

Sorry. Shall we begin?

SHARON

That would be so helpful.

WYATT

Then let us delay no longer. Let us sweep into action with nary a moment's hesitation.

HE claps his hands.

Now!

Short pause.

WYATT (CONT'D)

The word "Renaissance." What does it mean?

SHARON

Oh! I explain that on page—

WYATT

No.

SHARON

—two, I think, and three—

WYATT holds up his hand. Pause.

WYATT

Just a moment. I'm asking a straightforward question. I'm not looking for quotations. I can find those myself. This is just a straightforward question. What does the word "Renaissance" mean?

A beat.

SHARON

It means "rebirth."

WYATT

That's right. It means "rebirth." Not hard, was it?

SHARON

I wasn't aware you were asking such a simple question—

WYATT

Simple question! Sometimes those questions are the most difficult. Often it's the simple questions that probe to the essence of a problem.

WYATT (CONT'D)
(a beat)
Simplicity is in itself an art.
(short pause)
Or were you suggesting something else?

SHARON
Pardon me?

WYATT
You weren't suggesting that I was being simple.

SHARON
Perhaps that was an unfortunate phrase–

WYATT
Not perhaps. It was an unfortunate phrase.

> *From this point on, HE stands and strolls, then sits, then strolls.*

WYATT (CONT'D)
What I'm trying to do is clarify your terminology. And the question I'm raising by focusing on the literal meaning of "Renaissance," that is, "rebirth," is in reference to your specific use of that word in your title "The Elizabethan Renaissance." How are you using it? In what sense–

SHARON
As I said, I explain that on page–

WYATT
May I finish, please?

SHARON
I was only trying to help you understand–

WYATT
May I finish?

SHARON
I just wanted–

WYATT
May I finish?

SHARON
Sorry.

> *Pause.*

WYATT
You don't have to help me understand. I grasp the issues.
(short pause)
What I was trying to point out is that you treat all of the Renaissance as if it were a single movement, a monolithic structure.

WYATT (CONT'D)

Remember, it means "rebirth." Right? And a rebirth does not happen overnight, as you suggest. What, if I'm not being too simple, was it a rebirth of? Can you tell me?

SHARON

It was a rebirth of humanistic values, the interest in classical study that was allowed to lie dormant during the medieval ages–

WYATT

That's part of it–

SHARON

A renewed emphasis on humankind's temporal life as opposed to the spiritual–

WYATT

All right, all right!
(a beat)
You're talking in vague generalities here.

SHARON

You asked me a general question!

Pause.

WYATT

You have to differentiate among the various traditions of the time. Richard Hooker, for instance. Have you read Hooker?

SHARON

Not recently, I confess–

WYATT

You have to be right up on it. It's crucial to any project of this kind. Bodin of France?

SHARON

I've read him.

WYATT

In French, I assume.
(a beat)
I always prefer to read in the original, if only to maintain linguistic facility and thereby grasp subtleties of meaning, inflections, inevitably lost in any translation, no matter how felicitous it may appear.
(short pause)
Where were we?

SHARON

You were–

WYATT

Hooker and Bodin. Bodin and Hooker. Right.

> *Short pause.*

WYATT (CONT'D)

Of course, we cannot omit Castiglione in Italy. Castiglione and *The Book of the Courtier*. Castiglione and the glorious harmony of the mind and the body.

> *He flips through some pages.*

Do you mention him here?

SHARON

I don't believe so.

WYATT

What can I say?

> *(a beat)*

Sir Philip Sidney. *The Art of Poetry.* Nothing about him, as I recall.

> *SHARON shakes her head.*

You think I'm being too tough.

SHARON

I didn't say that–

WYATT

You see, in your attempt to provide a socio-political background against which to play out the drama of your dissertation, you group all of the figures of the time as if they were one man, one movement, one line of thought. But this is inaccurate. This is unscholarly. For, indeed, they are unique thinkers, with unique visions, unique approaches that you fail to distinguish–

SHARON

What I tried to do was single out one consistent line of Renaissance thought.

WYATT

But you can't–

SHARON

And I spent a whole chapter, thirty-five pages, organizing it. How much more can I do?

> *Pause.*

WYATT

May I speak?

> *SHARON nods.*

Are you in control?

> *Short pause.*

WYATT (CONT'D)

My dear young lady, please do not fall into the graduate student's classic pitfall. I've heard it so often. Whatever you do, do not confuse length and quality. That you spent thirty-five pages doing something, doing anything, is no guarantee that it is done properly.

SHARON

But it is well done.

WYATT

I disagree.

Short pause.

SHARON

All right. It has to be fixed. What would you suggest?

WYATT

That's what you should have been saying all along.

SHARON

I'm sorry, but–

WYATT

Do you want to argue with me? Must we reduce this conference to petty bickering? Or do you want my help in making this dissertation one of substance, something we can both be proud of?

(short pause)

After all, you have such potential. I'm sure we both have hopes for your future. I'd hate to see those put in jeopardy.

SHARON

I just want to get it finished! I've spent nearly three years on it!

(long pause)

WYATT

Now I'm going to say something. And I want you to listen carefully. Will you do that?

SHARON

Yes.

WYATT

Promise?

SHARON stares at him.

WYATT (CONT'D)

We don't grant the doctoral degree because people hang around here for a few years. I know other departments, other schools, where standards are slipping, and people get through for who knows what reason. But here a doctorate still means something. And I hope that when we do grant degrees, we grant them on one basis only. That basis is quality. Quality. That's what I expect from you. Okay?

Long pause.

SHARON

What do you want me to do?

WYATT

It's not what I *want* you to do. I'm only suggesting.

SHARON

What's the suggestion?

WYATT

Take your time. I'm willing to meet with you as often as necessary.

SHARON

What else?

WYATT

You have to develop the history of the Renaissance. Then move to Shakespeare and the specific texts under discussion. Your major problem is that you've failed to take into account the overall picture.

SHARON

I think I have taken it into account.

WYATT

Not to my way of thinking. And in the end, my way is the way that matters.

Pause.

SHARON

After all, it's supposed to be literary analysis, not history, and–

WYATT

I'm aware of your subject.

(short pause)

Sharon, what can I say? It's not easy for me to criticize you. But given my experience, and my understanding of the way things work around here, don't you think it might be wise to follow my advice? Don't you think it might be best, in the long run, to do this my way?

Pause.

SHARON

So far you've talked just about the introduction. Should I assume that's the only problem? If I include material about Hooker, Bodin, and *The Book of the Courtier*, will that do it?

WYATT

I wish I could say so. But I do see other trouble spots.

SHARON

I'm not sure what you mean–

WYATT
I'm talking about the entire structure of the dissertation, your methods of organization.
SHARON
That doesn't sound good.
WYATT
It isn't. You see, in each chapter, you take one major character: Viola, Rosalind, Desdemona, others–
SHARON
Cordelia, Imogen–
WYATT
I'm acquainted with the characters. Certainly restless this evening, aren't you?

(short pause)

Now.

HE flips through the manuscript.

I've lost the track here.
SHARON
You were talking about–
WYATT
There we are. The Renaissance. You see… you analyze each of these characters according to this general scheme you set up. Of course, the Renaissance section is not developed properly right now, as I've said, and as I think you agree–
SHARON
I know that part already!

Pause.

WYATT
My dear, I know you *think* you know. I know you *think* everything is clear. I know you *think* this should all go quickly. I know you *think* you understand–
SHARON
Go ahead–
WYATT
But there are points of concern to me–
SHARON
I know–
WYATT
Points of which you must be made aware! Is that clear?

SHARON

Yes.

WYATT

I won't have to say it again.

SHARON

No.

WYATT

Good.

(short pause)

Sharon, I know how much this work means to you. Still, we must maintain discipline, irrespective of personal feelings.

Pause.

SHARON

You were speaking about the construction of the dissertation. Could you explain further?

WYATT

All right. You set up each character against the background of his world–

SHARON

Her world.

WYATT

May I go on?

(short pause)

But here is the crucial matter. To what end? That is the question. To what end? You tell plots. All right. Not necessary, but you do it with some efficiency, although I wish you had not done it at all. Then you analyze each character.

Pause.

SHARON

I was simply attempting to–

WYATT

It doesn't matter what you were attempting! What you have done is useless. You offer no comparisons, no contrasts, no relationships between characters. Merely plot. Which does not amount to a dissertation. Am I making myself clear?

SHARON raises her hand.

WYATT (CONT'D)

No need to be formal. Speak right up.

SHARON

I confess this strikes me a bit strange.

WYATT
I understand. No writer likes to be criticized–
SHARON
That's not–
WYATT
We all take pride in our work.
SHARON
I don't–
WYATT
I remember a problem I had with an article of mine, one, in fact, the editor had requested. Then he turned around and rejected the thing–
SHARON
Pardon me, but may I establish *my* point?

Pause.

WYATT
What would you like to say?
SHARON

My idea for construction came from another dissertation.
WYATT
Oh, bad move, very bad move. Surely you know how many inferior products sneak through. Careless, poorly considered, highly unreliable–
SHARON
It was your dissertation.

Pause.

WYATT
Are you trying to be smart?
SHARON
Of course not.
WYATT
Are you spying on me?
SHARON
Not at all–
WYATT
Because your remark could be taken that way–
SHARON
I was just reading up on various dissertations, looking for inspiration.

Short pause.

WYATT
I suppose there are similarities—
SHARON
Quite a few—
WYATT
Although I suspect most are merely surface—
SHARON
"Heroes of Elizabethan Revenge Drama," right?
WYATT
Very flattering—
SHARON
We use the same construction: some background, each major character, and a conclusion.
WYATT
I remember!

(short pause)

WYATT (CONT'D)
You realize, of course, that my work has nothing to do with your situation. The circumstances are entirely different.
SHARON
I don't see—
WYATT
The schools are different—
SHARON
Just a minute—
WYATT
The times are different—
SHARON
What does that have to do—
WYATT
I'm afraid, and I know this will sound cruel, that nothing changes the fact that your work lacks organization! And no amount of whining on your part can do away with that problem!
SHARON
I am not whining!
WYATT
Sounds that way to me.
SHARON
I am only pointing out—

WYATT
There's no use in raving—
SHARON
Listen to me—
WYATT
Because the inescapable fact is that whatever I did is of no concern to you.
SHARON
All I want to say is that your dissertation—
WYATT
No concern at all.
SHARON
I just wanted to say—
WYATT
No concern at all!
(short pause)
Clear?
(short pause)
Good. Then let's move to our next topic. Diction. Language.
SHARON
What do you mean?
WYATT
Syntax.
SHARON
I'm not sure...
WYATT
Are you serious? A scholar like yourself? You don't recognize these terms?
SHARON
Of course I do—
WYATT
Then you seize my meaning. Your diction, language, and syntax are improper.
SHARON
Where?
WYATT
Through and through. The dissertation is badly marred, even fatally so, by substandard writing.
SHARON
Could you give me an example?

WYATT

You want me to amplify?

SHARON

You'd better.

WYATT

Then here we go.

HE flips through the pages.

Anywhere around here. Just a minute. Ah! For instance, you write "Rosalind is perhaps Shakespeare's most undiluted paradigm of dynamic feminism." What kind of writing is that?

SHARON

What's wrong with it?

WYATT

You must be joking.

SHARON

What's wrong with it?

WYATT

Why do you use the word "undiluted"? It certainly doesn't belong in this context. And what in the world is "dynamic feminism"?

SHARON

The meaning–

WYATT

Is this in some way the opposite of "undynamic feminism"? Can we have an "enervated feminism"?

SHARON

The meaning is perfectly clear–

WYATT

Please, no explanations.

SHARON

If you look at the overall context–

WYATT

I don't want explanations–

SHARON

I'm just trying to–

WYATT

No explanations–

SHARON

The point is–

WYATT
No explanations! Don't give me an oral report. Everything has to be written down. It should be clear without your amending commentaries.

SHARON
But it is clear, if you'll only look–

WYATT
Dear, dear, Sharon, it is not clear–

SHARON
It *is* clear–

WYATT
No, it is *not* clear!
(short pause)
And this is only one example. Do you need more?

SHARON
I don't see why you think that this section–

WYATT
I can give you more.

SHARON
Let me just show you–

WYATT
Do I have to?

SHARON
All I'm saying is that–

WYATT
Do I have to give you more?
(short pause)
Let's just say that the language is weak throughout. Can we agree on that?

SHARON
If you insist.

WYATT
I do. And there you have it.

> *HE tosses the dissertation onto the hassock. Short pause.*

SHARON
Nothing else?

WYATT
Those would qualify as the salient weaknesses.

SHARON
I don't know what I'm left with.

WYATT
A good deal of work, I should think.
> *HE kicks the hassock towards her.*

SHARON
A good deal.

WYATT
I don't want to be accused of underestimating the task.

SHARON
I have to rewrite the whole thing–

WYATT
You're being overemotional.
> *HE stands and looks out the window.*

I certainly hope it doesn't rain. Sometimes those roads become impossible–

SHARON
I've put in three years on this thing. On top of three years of graduate school even before I started it.

WYATT
Seems to be getting longer all the time. Still, nothing out of the ordinary there. You're seeking the doctorate, the terminal degree, the recognition by the scholarly community of your expertise–

SHARON
I have an interesting, original topic that I have explored in scholarly fashion–

WYATT
Let's not become excessively enthusiastic.

SHARON
The study of women characters is, as you expressed it, fertile field.

WYATT
In most cases, yes, but like everything else in Shakespeare already the subject of the most exhaustive analysis, most of which you ignore.

SHARON
I do nothing of the kind! My bibliography–

WYATT
My dear girl–

SHARON
My bibliography is twenty-three pages long, covering books and articles on every aspect of–

WYATT
My dear girl, once again–

SHARON

Will you stop that paternalistic condescension!

Long pause.

WYATT

As I was saying, your research is shoddy. Have you read, for instance, T. R. Robertson's 1962 study, S*hakespeare's Women*?

SHARON

No. I haven't managed to cover every single–

WYATT

One of the seminal works in your field. Crucial. Absolutely.

SHARON

I can't read everything.

WYATT

The graduate student's eternally feeble excuse. This *is* the time to read everything. If not now, when?

(short pause)

I'll try something more contemporary. Have you considered Cooper's latest article in *NERA*?

SHARON

What's *NERA*?

WYATT

The *New England Renaissance Annual.* Certainly one of our more important scholarly journals.

SHARON

I've never heard of it.

WYATT

Hardly a sign of mastery. Then I gather you have not read Phil Cooper's article therein.

SHARON

No.

WYATT

A profound study, I assure you. But if you didn't see that one, you must have missed one of my own reviews in the same issue.

SHARON

I'm afraid so.

WYATT

(standing and walking)

Fine book on John Marston. I did an article on him for *NERA*, and Phil asked me to write the review.

SHARON

What do you mean, he asked you?

WYATT

Phil's the editor. The journal's published at his school, and he chooses the contributors. I must have reprints around here somewhere. Remind me to give you one before you leave.

HE begins to rummage.

SHARON

And why is the article by... Cooper, is that his name?

WYATT

Phil Cooper. Top man.

SHARON

Why is it so important?

WYATT

He says essentially what you do about the women of the festive comedies in one-quarter the words. Of course, he does lack your bubble and charm.

SHARON

My bubble and charm are not in question.

WYATT

In fact, in the same issue there's another article that should give you pause. Somewhere in your dissertation... I forget where... you mention imagery of flowers. Am I right?

SHARON

In the chapter on *A Midsummer Night's Dream*–

WYATT

Wherever. In *NERA* Henry Hollings has a terribly good piece that ought to be of great concern to you: "The Flowering of Mind: Memory, Poetry, and Shrubbery." Need I continue?

SHARON

You've made your point.

WYATT

It's worth restating. Your scholarship is shoddy, embarrassingly so. And no amount of crying about the years you have devoted–

SHARON

I am not crying–

WYATT

No amount of crying will excuse that deficiency.

Pause.

SHARON

Can I ask you one more thing?

WYATT

Is there any point?

SHARON

Just one?

WYATT

You're getting carried away by emotion. You take these things so personally—

SHARON

Listen to one passage—

WYATT

No need.

SHARON

Just one!

WYATT

I don't think so.

SHARON

Will you tell me what's wrong with one passage—

WYATT

I don't have to go into specifics.

SHARON

Just listen!

WYATT

I don't care to.

Pause.

SHARON

What'd you think of Chapter Seven?

WYATT

Hmmm?

SHARON

Chapter Seven. What'd you think of it?

WYATT

Which one was that?

SHARON

The chapter on the Romances. What did you think of it?

WYATT

Hard to say.

SHARON

But you must have some opinion.

WYATT
Nothing special. Same as the others. Same problems. Needs rewriting, restructuring, new research. New approach altogether.
SHARON
What about my thesis in that chapter?
WYATT
Again, it's hard to specify. Same problems all along.
SHARON
Can't you offer a single detail? Did you think any of the points original?
WYATT
They made little impression–
SHARON
Don't you have anything to add?
WYATT
I've made my position clear–
SHARON
Did you read this?

Pause.
WYATT
Pardon me?

Long pause.
SHARON
How long will it take?
WYATT
To what are you referring?
SHARON
If I go back to work and resubmit it, how long before you pass it?
WYATT
Quality cannot be rushed.
SHARON
How long?
WYATT
As I'm trying to indicate–
SHARON
How long?
WYATT
That's not easy to determine.

SHARON

How long?

WYATT

It's difficult to gauge these things in actual time. I realize you're certainly anxious, or should I say eager—

SHARON

How much do you want?

WYATT

Please don't make it sound so crass. After all, we're dealing on a scholarly plane—

SHARON

How much... do you want?

Pause.

WYATT

Well... clearly what we call "major revisions" are in order. And those can last from as little as a few months to... oh... a year or two.

SHARON

A year or two.

WYATT

With steady effort. Impossible to say precisely.
(short pause)
I must say, though, that sometimes the problems have been worked out to everyone's satisfaction much more quickly.

Long pause.

SHARON

I was about to get Professor Hagen's signature on this dissertation. In fact, if he hadn't left, I wouldn't be with you now.

WYATT

It's always awkward to lose an advisor. Although let's remind ourselves that his approval would not have carried much weight in the academic community. After all, how seriously can we take an instructor who gives A's to an entire class, including some dozen students who never even showed up?

SHARON

I'm not responsible for his behavior.

WYATT

He just strolled out of the room, didn't he? And now he's on a walking tour of Ecuador.

SHARON

I am not responsible—

WYATT

Inspiring. Anyway, I wouldn't boast about his approbation. It came awfully easily.

Pause.

SHARON

I'll ask once more: what do I have to do?

WYATT

I wish you wouldn't put it so coarsely.

SHARON

I have to get your signature on this dissertation. What do I have to do?

WYATT

We mustn't forget your other reader, who is...

SHARON

Professor Twilley.

WYATT

Ah, Twilley! And what does he have to say?

SHARON

He claims he hasn't had time to read it yet.

WYATT

Is that so?

SHARON

But everyone knows the truth. He's coming up for tenure, so he'll do whatever you want.

WYATT

I think you're overdramatizing my authority. True, I'll fight hard for you, as I would for any student in whom I believe–

SHARON

Whatever you say goes.

Short pause.

WYATT

Heavy responsibility. Makes a man feel... humble.

SHARON

Tell me exactly what you want.

Pause.

WYATT

I think tonight has been a difficult experience for you. You're overwrought. And in no mood to... work things out. We ought to get together on another occasion.

SHARON

When?

WYATT

No reason to dawdle.

SHARON

When?

WYATT

Why don't I leave that up to you? This is, as always, a busy time of year, but I'll fit you in.

> *SHARON picks up her bag and the dissertation, then walks to the door.*

WYATT (CONT'D)

In the meantime, reflect on what I've said. Think about the construction of the dissertation, the introduction, the–

SHARON

I'm not giving up.

WYATT

I don't expect you to. Because up to now we've enjoyed such–

> *SHE slams the door behind her. Pause.*

WYATT (CONT'D)

–a pleasant relationship.

> *HE shrugs, sits, and resumes reading.*

END OF ACT ONE

ACT TWO

SCENE ONE

THREE EVENINGS LATER.

WYATT is at his desk, rummaging. The doorbell rings.

WYATT

Yeah!

HE goes to the door and opens it to reveal SHARON, who wears a short skirt, a blouse, and high-heeled shoes. SHE carries her dissertation and her shoulder bag.

SHARON

Am I allowed in?

WYATT

Please.

As HE motions her in, SHE enters. HE closes the door.

SHARON

I hope you don't mind my showing up suddenly.

WYATT

Not at all.

HE studies her.

We certainly did get that rain, didn't we?

SHARON

Wasn't that something? It really poured.

WYATT

I knew it'd get sloppy out there. Some of those walkways have turned to mud.

SHARON

It is a mess.

WYATT

Still, no reason to bring it in here.

SHARON

I beg your pardon?

WYATT snaps his fingers and points at her shoes.

SHARON (CONT'D)

Should I take them off?

WYATT

I do have a woman who comes in every week. And she's a good worker. But I hardly think it fair that she should have to clean up after you as well as me.

SHARON

I didn't bring any others.

WYATT

I pride myself on maintaining a casual ambience.

SHARON steps out of her shoes.

SHARON

By the door okay?

WYATT

Fine.

SHARON places her shoes next to the door.

WYATT (CONT'D)

Thank you. Now, what's up?

SHARON

I don't want to take a lot of your time. I know how busy you are.

WYATT

Quite all right.

WYATT points to the sofa, and SHARON walks over and sits. HE sits in his chair.

SHARON

You're being very kind about this.

WYATT

About what?

SHARON

Well… first I want to apologize about the other night. I'm so embarrassed.

WYATT

As I indicated, I know this is a tough time for you.

SHARON

So you said, but–

WYATT

I understand, believe me.

SHARON

Please. I have to say this.

WYATT gestures that SHE should continue.

Last week I acted just like the kind of person I hate. Like a spoiled little girl.

WYATT
You might have been a bit rash—
SHARON
Petulant—
WYATT
Headstrong, perhaps—
SHARON
I almost threw a tantrum! I was awful!

Short pause.

WYATT
You do have a few things to learn about academic decorum—
SHARON
I know, I know! I came here assuming everything I did was so wonderful—
WYATT
It's easy to get carried away.
SHARON
That's what happened! I was sure you were going to fall all over yourself telling me how brilliant I was!
WYATT
As I say, you're under a lot of pressure—
SHARON
Even so, I should never have been so rude! That was unforgivable!
WYATT
I think we've established that it was not one of your better evenings.
SHARON
Agreed.

(a beat)

Of course, when I got home, I considered what you had said. That's when I realized you were only thinking of me. Although that wasn't easy to admit.
WYATT
It never is.
SHARON
But as long as you're willing to forgive me for acting like such a child...
WYATT
(miming absolution)
Consider yourself forgiven.
SHARON
Then it was worth saying.

SHARON (CONT'D)
(a beat)
I might as well say something else, too. I'm quite aware that after you've approved my dissertation, people will know what kind of project it must be and the kind of work I can do. I mean, it'll be nice when Professor Twilley likes it, but, let's face it. He isn't of your stature. And I should have been aware of that the other night, too.

WYATT
Very generous. And obviously you're right.

HE laughs. SHE joins in.

WYATT (CONT'D)
One more thing. Having a good dissertation carries weight when you're on the lookout for a job.

SHARON
Does it? I wasn't sure.

WYATT
Strong recommendations on top of a strong dissertation. That's how you move up.
(a beat)
Oh, there's politics involved, as you well know—

SHARON
We hear a lot of rumors—

WYATT
My dear girl— Oh, I'm sorry. You're not fond of that expression.

SHARON
Such a silly point. What's all the fuss about?

WYATT
I don't know, but the other night you were—

SHARON
I'd prefer to forget about the other night, if that's all right. I wasn't myself.

WYATT
Not another word.

SHARON
Thanks! Anyway, you were telling me about…

WYATT
Right, right. Hirings and firings based on nothing but politics. Politics, petty hatreds, and jealousies. And favors. Plenty of favors. Believe me, it isn't always quality that wins the day.

SHARON
Sounds pretty discouraging.

WYATT
And I worry about it.
(a beat)
By the way, I could tell you something about Twilley, if you want a laugh.

SHARON
No! Not...

WYATT
That's right. Dynamite himself. When he came here for his interview, no one was impressed. I presume that doesn't surprise you.

SHARON
He is... quiet.

WYATT
I would've said "drippy."

SHARON laughs.

WYATT (CONT'D)
But somebody at Twilley's school knew somebody here, and somebody here owed somebody there, so most of us went along. No one was too happy. But that's the way the system works. I'm afraid we live in a community that is something less than the pillar of virtue people imagine. I'll tell you stories sometime.

SHARON
I'll look forward to it. I think!

THEY laugh. Pause.

Well...

SHE begins to gather her things.

WYATT
Leaving so soon?

SHARON
I don't want to intrude any more–

WYATT
But you've brought your dissertation.

SHARON
Oh, boy! I almost forgot!

WYATT
Did you want something? Did you have a question?

SHARON
I did! But I guess I'm just so glad we're friends again.

WYATT
Sit down! Let's talk it over!

SHARON

As long as I'm not taking you away from something more important.

WYATT

Nothing's more important than my students.

SHARON

Great!

SHE struggles with her dissertation.

Heavy!

WYATT

Because it's full of weighty ideas!

SHE laughs. HE smiles.

SHARON

Anyway, I've done some rethinking.

SHE sits on the floor, next to the hassock.

WYATT

Good!

SHARON

Let's hope! The other night you suggested that I approach my work from a... different angle. And I'm ready to do that.

SHE stretches out beside him.

WYATT

Delighted.

SHARON

And I'm hoping you'll look at one or two sections and be even more specific.

WYATT

Why don't we read it together?

SHARON

All right!

HE picks up the dissertation.

SHARON (CONT'D)

And you can tell me just what you want.

WYATT

Good enough.

SHE smiles and extends her legs near him.

Let's see.

HE begins reading, while he glances at her body.

Hm-mm.

HE flips through the first few pages.

WYATT (CONT'D)

You know, it's funny. The other night I had quite a few complaints about this introduction...

SHARON

And I'm sure you were right.

WYATT

And yet, as I read it again, with fresh eyes... this seems stronger than I initially thought.

SHARON

Does it really?

WYATT

This section does, at any rate. It's crisp, clear.

HE looks at her legs.

Well supported.

HE reads.

What can I say? I may have been hasty.

HE shakes his head.

You know, professors aren't flawless. Sometimes we have a tendency to blow things out of proportion.

SHARON

That was probably my fault. I was making everything so difficult for you.

WYATT

No, no. I lost sight of things. I was focusing on details and lost the big picture.

HE looks at her legs.

As the saying goes, I may have missed the forest for the trees. A good part of this, perhaps most of it, is definitely salvageable.

SHARON

That's wonderful!

WYATT

Tell you what. I'm in the mood to get right to it. How about you?

HE closes the dissertation and pats the hassock.

SHARON

Ready on this end.

SHE moves onto the hassock.

WYATT

Then I think we're headed for a lot of progress.

SHARON

You can't imagine how happy this makes me.

SHE kisses his cheek, then withdraws.

SHARON (CONT'D)

Oh, I'm sorry!

SHE stands.

Please forgive me. I was so excited!

SHE walks back to the sofa and sits. Pause.

WYATT

Don't worry about it.

HE puts the dissertation aside.

After all, we're not only colleagues. We're friends.

HE walks toward her.

And friends should be… comfortable with each other.

HE sits next to her and takes her hand.

And a kiss between friends is… perfectly fine.

HE kisses her. SHE moves slightly away.

SHARON

Wow! If we're going to be working for two more years, we'd better go a little slower.

WYATT

Two years? Why two years?

SHARON

The other night that's how long you said it might take.

WYATT

I know, but–

SHARON

Of course, I'm hoping that if I work hard…

WYATT

That goes without saying. And if we work together, really focusing our energies…

HE pulls her to him.

And do everything we can to help you…

SHARON

Then maybe we're not rushing matters after all.

WYATT

My thoughts exactly.

THEY kiss.

END OF SCENE ONE

SCENE TWO

THREE WEEKS LATER. EVENING.

WYATT is in his chair, drinking. The doorbell rings. HE checks his watch, puts down his drink, and opens the door. SHARON enters. SHE grabs him around the neck and kisses him.

SHARON
And how are you tonight?

SHE takes off her shoes and tosses them across the room, then settles on the sofa.

WYATT
Suddenly in much better spirits.

HE sits next to her.

Was it my imagination, or was I supposed to call you?

SHARON
Does it matter? You looked so lonely when I passed by your office today.
(a beat)
Especially when that book representative left.

WYATT
I told you. She's a former student. I couldn't just throw her out.

SHARON
Sure, sure.

WYATT
I promise. There's nothing–

SHARON
Can't you tell when I'm kidding? I know it was just business.

WYATT
That's what I figured.

SHARON
But you definitely need to relax. That's why this is a perfect night for a celebration.

SHE embraces him.

WYATT
Not that I'm objecting, you understand, but what are we celebrating?

SHARON
Isn't any signing of a dissertation cause for a party?

WYATT
That's a fair assumption.

SHARON

And after all we've done, and your extraordinary exertions on my behalf...

WYATT

I've enjoyed every minute of it.

SHARON

I'll bet you have.

SHE kisses him.

Anyway, thank you. And I am proud to say that it's ready now, isn't it?

WYATT

Let me put it this way. I have never seen major revisions handled so efficiently.

SHARON

I couldn't have done it without you.

WYATT

My pleasure. Certainly my perspective on the material has changed. I think it stands as a significant contribution.

SHARON

That makes me feel almost as good as something else will later tonight. In fact, I've been dreaming about it all day.

WYATT

To what are you alluding?

SHARON

Don't be coy.

WYATT

I haven't the slightest idea what you mean.

SHARON

I believe you referred to it the other evening as "Journey to the Center of the Earth."

SHE lies back.

WYATT

Oh. That.

SHARON

Oh. That.

HE leans over her, but SHE holds him away with her foot.

SHARON (CONT'D)

Business before pleasure.

HE kisses her foot.

WYATT

Then why don't I find your dissertation before we go any further?

SHARON

What a marvelous idea.

> *WYATT goes to his desk and looks through the pile of papers and binders.*

That's mine. Right there.

> *WYATT picks up a binder.*

WYATT

I'm not likely to forget this one.

SHARON

I should hope not. Need a pen?

WYATT

Have one right here.

> *HE picks up a pen.*

SHARON

Then bring it all over.

> *SHE pats the sofa.*

I want to watch.

> *WYATT brings the dissertation and sits next to her.*

SHARON

Isn't this exciting?

> *SHE moves close to him.*

WYATT

Always a memorable occasion.

SHARON

Especially tonight. With you.

> *SHE kisses him.*

WYATT

And you.

> *HE kisses her.*

Here we go.

> *HE opens the binder and takes his pen.*

Don't forget, though: a few steps remain.

SHARON

Twilley, for one.

WYATT
And you do have to defend this before a committee. I suspect you'll need some private preparation for that.
SHARON
I wonder who I should work with? Hmmm.
WYATT
He'll have to be special.
SHARON
Oh, I'll think of someone. And that means we still have a long way to go together.

SHE cradles his face. THEY kiss.

WYATT
So we do. Ready?

HE holds up the pen, poised to sign.

SHARON
Ready.

HE opens the dissertation and signs it.

WYATT
There. All approved. How do you feel?

HE puts down the pen.

SHARON
I can't believe it. I've waited so long.
WYATT
You should feel very proud.
SHARON
I couldn't have done it without you.

SHE puts the dissertation aside, then begins to unbutton his shirt.

WYATT
What's going on?
SHARON
I think it's time to reward you for a job well done.
WYATT
I can't wait.
SHARON
I have only one more favor.
WYATT
What would you like?

SHARON
Just one.

WYATT
Name it.

SHARON
Talk to Twilley.

WYATT
I don't think there's any need.

SHARON
Do it anyway.

WYATT
Why?

SHARON
Because I saw him today. And he still hasn't finished reading.

WYATT
He might be busy.

SHARON
That's what I thought. But I have a feeling it's something else.

WYATT
How do you know?

SHARON
I don't think he likes it.

WYATT
Did he say something?

SHARON
I just have a feeling.

WYATT
Did he say something?

SHARON
Not in so many words.

WYATT
Then there's nothing to worry about.

SHARON
I think there is.

WYATT
Are you doubting me?

SHARON
Of course not!

WYATT
I told you. I'll take care of it.

SHARON
But he's taking an awfully long time.

WYATT
Not really. Besides, I told you. I'm in charge here.

SHARON
That's fine, but–

WYATT
I've got it under control. You'll just have to be little more patient.

SHARON
Listen–

WYATT
He won't dare go against me. Clear?

SHARON
Yes, but–

WYATT
Clear?

Short pause.

SHARON
The thing is, I'm tired of waiting. And you can handle Twilley.

WYATT
I don't want to overdo it. I'd prefer to give him a few more days.

SHARON
I'd prefer that you didn't. You said you're in charge. Then show me. He needs to be pushed. Push him.

WYATT
It may not be the right move.

SHARON
Push him.

WYATT
Are you sure you want me to?

SHARON
Push him.

SHE pushes him down.

Just the thought of it arouses me.

Short pause.

WYATT
I'll talk to him tomorrow.

SHARON
How can I thank you?
WYATT
You know.
SHARON
Then relax. And put yourself in my hands.
SHE clasps his hands, and their fingers interlock.
WYATT
Once more unto the breach, dear friends…
SHE kisses him.
END OF SCENE TWO

SCENE THREE

A WEEK LATER. EVENING.

WYATT is at the bar, a drink in his hand. The doorbell rings. HE puts down the drink, goes to the door, and opens it.

SHARON

It's me!

WYATT

What are you… ?

SHARON

How ya' doin'!

SHE enters carrying a shoulder bag and a stuffed animal, and dragging two suitcases.

Surprised to see me, right? And I'll bet you're even more surprised to see me with these!

SHE shoves the stuffed animal at him. HE grasps it.

WYATT

I confess I am—

SHARON

Do I have news for you! Just let me put my things in the bedroom.

SHE drags the suitcases towards the bedroom.

WYATT

Wait a minute—

SHARON
(Going off)

Be right there!

WYATT closes the door. HE tosses the stuffed animal aside. SHARON returns.

SHARON (CONT'D)

I'll get the rest later.

WYATT

The rest of what?

SHARON

You're not gonna believe what's happened.

As SHE passes WYATT, SHE kisses him enthusiastically. HE barely reacts. SHE collapses on the sofa.

SHARON (CONT'D)
Wow! Let me take a breath!
WYATT
What exactly is going on?
SHARON
Sit down, and I'll tell you all about it!

SHE pats the sofa. HE still stands.

WYATT
I'm waiting.
SHARON
Did you hear about Twilley?
WYATT
No.
SHARON
You didn't?
WYATT
No.
SHARON
He didn't call you?
WYATT
No! What's going on?
SHARON
Oh, boy! Get ready for a story.
(a beat)
I'm telling you. You'd better sit down.

WYATT stands still.

SHARON (CONT'D)
All right. Last Tuesday I went to see him.
WYATT
But I've already talked to him. Twice!
SHARON
I know. And I'm so grateful for the support you've given me throughout this entire matter—
WYATT
What about Twilley?
SHARON
Well... it seems he's decided that he doesn't have time to be one of my readers.

WYATT

No *time*?!

SHARON

That's what he said.

WYATT

What's he talking about? It doesn't take any time! You just sign the thing!

HE goes to the bar.

SHARON

He said he had to do some extra reading and research, but I think he was trying to pull a fast one.

WYATT

That twit! Of course he was! What'd you say?

SHARON

I asked who was going to take his place.

WYATT

And what'd he say?

SHARON

He said he didn't know. Said he was going to leave the whole matter with the Chair of the Department.

WYATT

Roy?

SHARON

Right.

WYATT puts down his drink.

WYATT

All right. I can talk to him.

SHARON

'Fraid it's a little late for that.

WYATT

What do you mean?

(a beat)

What!?

SHARON

You sure you don't want to sit down?

WYATT

Just tell me!

SHARON

Roy… Professor Thatcher… has already made his decision.

WYATT

And?

SHARON

Yesterday morning I got an e-mail.

> *Short pause.*

WYATT

From whom?

SHARON

Should I get you a drink?

WYATT

From *whom*?

SHARON

From my new reader.
> *(a beat)*

Nan Blocker.

> *WYATT sits on the end of the sofa.*

WYATT

Oh, God.

SHARON

That's what I said.

WYATT

Why did he appoint her?

SHARON

Who knows?

> *Short pause.*

WYATT

All right. When did she say she'd get to it?

SHARON

I saw her this morning. She's finished it.

WYATT

And?

SHARON

You won't believe it.
> *(a beat)*

She hates what we did.

WYATT

Oh, no.

> *HE moves to the hassock.*

SHARON
She gave me a whole list of things. Bad construction. Poor research. She thought the intellectual background of the Renaissance was completely inadequate. She even said a good deal of the writing was weak.
(a beat)
And I thought we had it all fixed up.
Short pause.
WYATT
We may have rushed.
SHARON
She even used the word "drivel."
(a beat)
Does she have anything against you? I mean, she was really nasty.
WYATT
I don't know what she thinks.
SHARON
And she got specific, too.
SHE stands and strolls.
WYATT
What do you mean?
SHARON
Lots of things. Like we never should have bothered with Castiglione. Instead we should have emphasized Sir Thomas More. And we should have covered the Puritans, with their doctrines about marriage and the legal status of women. And women's place in the community.
WYATT
That stuff goes on forever!
SHARON
She also said I should have written about chastity.
WYATT
Chastity!?
SHARON
Can you believe it?
WYATT
What about chastity?
SHARON
All the moral, social, political, and theological implications. In fact, she said there's a whole range of materials about women that we've ignored completely.

WYATT
Oh, God.

SHARON
You'll talk to her, won't you?

WYATT
I can try, but–

SHARON
Do you want to look at the list?

WYATT
What I want to know is why she's sticking her nose into this! What business is it of hers? Anyway, I thought we had gotten rid of her.

SHARON
Not until the end of the year. And she's given me so much to cover. I don't know how I'm going to do it all.

WYATT
You'll have to.

SHARON
I'm not sure I can.

WYATT
It may take a while.

SHARON
She called it "major revisions."

WYATT
Nothing you can do but go to work.

SHARON
Uh-huh.
(a beat)
But there's another problem.

WYATT
What now?

SHARON
It's the reason I brought over my suitcases. My lease is up. And I don't have anywhere to go.

WYATT
What are you talking about?

SHARON
A few weeks ago, after you signed my dissertation, I figured I had the degree wrapped up. So I told my landlord I was leaving. Now I'm out.

WYATT

But there must be somewhere you can go.

SHARON

There probably is. But I don't have any money.

WYATT

What about friends? I know you have plenty of those.

SHARON shakes her head.

WYATT (CONT'D)

Can't your family help?

SHARON

No way.

SHE pushes him so that HE falls into his chair.

Sweetheart, I have to stay here.

WYATT

There's no room!

SHARON

How much space could I take? Besides, I'll be in the library all day. The only time we'd be together is at night.

SHE moves close to him.

We'll set records.

SHE kisses him.

Besides, it'd only be for six weeks or so.

WYATT

Six weeks? How can you do it all so fast?

SHE sits on the hassock.

SHARON

Well, believe it or not, something else has come up: the possibility of a job offer.

WYATT

Really!

SHARON

I guess it's not bad luck to talk about it.

WYATT

Let's hear it.

SHARON

Well, you know Harry Conklin. He's Chairman–

WYATT

I know him!

SHARON

Not one of your great friends?

WYATT

How do you know that?

SHARON

Well, somebody told me that you once had a fight with him—

WYATT

Never mind. Just tell me about the job.

SHARON

Sorry. Anyway, you're not going to believe it! The irony of it all.

WYATT

Yeah. Tell me about the irony.

SHARON

It's amazing! He and I have known each other for… oh, a long time. And he's always had an interest in my work. Even told me how wonderful it would be for me to join his Department. Well, suddenly they have an opening. Beginning in February. And I applied. And what do you know? Harry told me that I was the top candidate for the job.

WYATT

Fine! You'll join up with him, live there, teach, earn your money, finish your degree… eventually… and you'll be all set.

SHARON

But there's one hitch.

WYATT

What?

SHARON

He can't appoint me yet.

WYATT

Why not?

SHARON

His Dean is one of those real sticklers, and insists that all the full-time people they appoint have a Ph.D.

WYATT

So?

SHARON

So unless I get the degree in the next couple of months, I lose the job.

WYATT

And the money.

SHARON
And the place to live. But if I get the degree, I start there in February. Harry's guaranteed that.

WYATT
He's certainly helpful.

SHARON
He's been very kind.

WYATT
Maybe, but be careful. He's a sleazy guy.

SHARON
I'll watch him every step.
(a beat)
Still, I don't know what to do. If I don't get the degree, I don't get the job. And if I don't get the job now, who knows when an opportunity will come again? And as much as I hate to be a burden to you, where else can I stay?

WYATT
Sharon—

SHARON
Yet I can't help imagining the fun we'll have.

WYATT
Wait a minute!

SHARON
What?

WYATT
People visit this house all the time.

SHARON
What people?

WYATT
Colleagues. Students.
(a beat)
Friends.

SHARON
So? I probably know most of 'em.

WYATT
Exactly. That's why explaining what you're doing here might be awkward.

SHARON
Would it really?

WYATT
Well…

SHARON
Because we're certainly not doing anything wrong, are we?

WYATT
No, but...

SHARON
Besides, now your friends can meet my friends. We'll expand our circles.

WYATT
Yeah, but...

SHARON
But what?

WYATT
There's no room for your furniture.

SHARON
Oh It's going into storage. I have just enough money for that.

WYATT
And you figure you can get all the work done in such a short time?

SHARON
I'm sure gonna try.

SHE moves beside him.

SHARON (CONT'D)
Besides, darling, your reputation's on the line. And I'll be darned if I'm going to let that go down the drain.

WYATT
My reputation!? What do I have to do with it?

SHARON
Well, sweetie, I'm sorry to put it this way, but isn't she... Nan Blocker... isn't she insulting you? I mean, here you are, a distinguished professor, and you've approved my work. And now here she comes, a nothing compared to you, a woman who's lost her job, and she's saying that what I've done is junk. I hate to say it, but she's implying that you don't know what you're talking about. That you're incompetent–

WYATT
I get the picture.

SHARON
She's publically demeaning you.

WYATT
I see it!

Short pause.

SHARON

So I figure I'll do all the work, and you'll check over what I'm doing. Just to make sure I'm on the right track—

WYATT

Look, I don't have time—

SHARON

Because the longer it takes me, the worse you look. And I would hate to have you seem like a fool in front of the entire Department.

Short pause.

WYATT

I'll help with what I can. But you'll have to do most of it.

SHARON

I'll do everything! Oh, I knew you'd never let me down.

SHE kisses him passionately.

Wow! Still the best!

WYATT

Thank you.

HE puts his feet on the hassock and picks up a magazine.

SHARON

Oh, by the way.

WYATT

What now?

SHARON

I almost hate to ask.

WYATT

What is it?!

SHARON

Another favor. Just a small one!

WYATT

You have my house. And I've promised to help! What more can I give you?

SHARON

Well, Blocker gave me an assignment for tomorrow.

WYATT

No problem. You have time.

SHARON

I need to get six articles from the library.

SHE takes out a sheet of paper.

WYATT
It's open 'til twelve.

SHARON
But I can't go.

WYATT
Why not?

SHARON
I have to clean out my apartment.

WYATT
Tonight?

SHARON
Otherwise I lose my deposit! They're coming tomorrow to take all my things!
(a beat)
Can you help me?

WYATT
How?

SHARON
Just this once… would you mind getting the articles for me?

WYATT
C'mon! It's late!

SHARON
But you'll do it so quickly! You know all the journals and everything! It won't take you any time at all!

WYATT
It's late!

SHE rubs against him.

SHARON
Please, please, please?
(a beat)
Here's the list.

SHE hands it to him. WYATT peruses it.

WYATT
It's all women's stuff!

SHARON
Right.

WYATT
Is this absolutely necessary?

SHARON

I don't want to get started off wrong with Nan.

Short pause.

WYATT

Nan.

SHARON

Uh-huh.

Short pause.

WYATT

All right. I can use the air.

HE stands.

But this is it.

SHARON

Absolutely.

WYATT

The dissertation has to be your work.

HE picks up his coat.

SHARON

I promise.

WYATT

I'm going to hold you to that.

HE opens the door.

SHARON

How can I thank you?

HE smiles.

WYATT

I'll think of something.

SHARON

And I'll expect to pay in full tonight.

SHE closes the door behind him. SHE walks to the bar and takes a drink. SHE goes to WYATT's chair, kicks of her shoes, puts her feet on the hassock, and smiles.

END OF SCENE THREE

SCENE FOUR

FIVE WEEKS LATER. EVENING.

SHARON is playing music and dancing. WYATT enters through the front door, exhausted. HE carries books from the library, as well as his briefcase. SHE dances over to him, takes him by the lapels, and tries to dance with him. HE stands still. SHE stops dancing and turns off the music. WYATT tosses his briefcase and the books aside, drops his coat, and flops on the sofa.

WYATT

I've had it.

SHARON

Tough day? I'm so sorry! Tell me what happened.

SHE sits on the sofa, puts his feet on her lap, and takes off his shoes.

WYATT

The Department meeting went on for hours. They kept talking and talking. About nothing!

SHARON

Isn't it always like that–

SHE strokes his feet.

WYATT

Then some guy came to my office to complain about an assignment. Said he was sick or something… I don't know.

HE kicks his feet free.

Hey! Just get me a drink, will you?

SHARON

Whatever you say.

SHE goes to the bar.

WYATT

This has been the longest semester of my life.

SHARON

Well, you've worked so hard.

SHE pours a drink for herself.

And I'm so appreciative.

SHE takes her drink to the chair and sits.

WYATT

Any word from Blocker? I saw her at the meeting, but she didn't say anything.

SHARON
I was keeping it a surprise. We talked today.

WYATT
When?

SHARON
This morning.

WYATT
Why didn't you call me?

SHARON
I couldn't reach you–

WYATT
I've been waiting!

SHARON
I tried three times, but–

WYATT
All right, all right! Never mind. What'd she say?

SHARON
I think you'll be pleased. First, she told me the whole dissertation was much improved. She was very impressed.

WYATT
I should hope so. I've spent more days in the library than I have in my office.

SHARON
I don't think it's the time that matters as much as the results. And they seem to be good.

WYATT
Finally! What is it, seventy new pages? Eighty?

SHARON
Something like that. The number doesn't really matter.

WYATT
Yeah. Okay, did she sign it?

SHARON
Well…

WYATT
What?
(a beat)
She didn't sign it?

SHARON
I feel terrible. Because I know how hard you've worked and the effort you've put in–

HE goes to the bar.

WYATT
What did she say?

SHARON
Well, as good as it is–

WYATT
What did she *say*?

SHARON
That some of our insights were intriguing. Very provocative.

HE pours a drink.

WYATT
What else?

SHARON
She was very complimentary–

WYATT
Sharon–

SHARON
But she still sees problems.

WYATT
What problems!?

SHARON
You're so tired. Don't you want to wait– ?

WYATT
What… *problems*?

HE slams the glass on the bar. Short pause.

SHARON
The introduction. It still isn't right–

WYATT
I rewrote the whole thing!

SHARON
And I thought it was wonderful! But Nan wasn't impressed.

WYATT
What's her complaint now?

SHARON

The background on the Renaissance still isn't right.

WYATT

What is the *matter* with her?

SHARON

She thinks there ought to be more on the international aspects. On the French influence as well as the German and Italian.

WYATT

Why?

SHARON

To provide a better link to the classical antecedents. She wants to emphasize the theme of rebirth.

WYATT

But all that's irrelevant! The dissertation is on Shakespeare.

SHARON

That's what I said.

WYATT

Good!

SHARON

Then she said she didn't need anyone to tell her about the nature of my topic.

WYATT

It will be a pleasure to say goodbye to her.

SHARON

At least there's one benefit to all this work with classical literature.

WYATT

What could possibly be a benefit?

SHARON

You'll maintain your fluency in Latin.

WYATT stares at her. Short pause.

WYATT

Is that it? Or does she have more?

SHARON looks at him. Pause.

WYATT (CONT'D)

More?

SHARON

She says she wants to uphold Departmental standards.

WYATT

I'm sick of her standards!

SHARON

But I guess her way is the way that counts, right?

HE sits on the sofa and sips his drink.

SHARON (CONT'D)

Okay. Back to work.

SHE claps her hands.

She still has difficulty with the structure.

WYATT

The structure! What's she talking about?

SHARON

You know. The organization of the dissertation.

WYATT

I know what structure is! I'm asking what's wrong with it!

SHARON

Apparently the chapters don't follow logically. At least according to Nan.

WYATT

Of course they do!

SHARON

Well, she said–

WYATT

The thing is perfectly constructed! It's just like mine!

Pause. SHARON stands.

SHARON

May I speak?

WYATT stares at her. Short pause.

Sweetheart, if you're going to keep whining…

WYATT

I am not whining!

SHARON

We'll never finish.

WYATT

I'm sorry!

SHARON

You're sure?

WYATT

Get on with it!

SHARON

Okay. She also said that in a few spots, the writing is still weak.

WYATT
Where?
SHARON
Different places.
WYATT
Couldn't she be specific?
SHARON
She said to check transitions and modifiers–
WYATT
I don't know what she means!
SHARON
You've never heard of those things?
WYATT
Of course I've heard of them! But if she's not going to give me examples–
SHARON
Darling...
WYATT
How am I supposed to correct what I don't see?

Short pause.

SHARON
You're getting much too emotional.
WYATT
I'm sorry!
SHARON
Sure you don't want to take a minute?
WYATT
I feel like I've been working on this thing for months!
SHARON
I know how tough it's been. But Nan says that in another few weeks we could finish.
WYATT
I don't have time! I have all my papers to correct!
SHARON
Darling...
WYATT
Plus I'm going to New Orleans for that symposium!
SHARON
You may have to cancel that.

WYATT

I can't!

SHARON

Then we'd better get to work.

WYATT

All right, all right! Go ahead!

SHARON

Thank you. Now, Chapter Four is still a problem.

WYATT

Four!? I fixed that one up just the way she wanted!

SHARON

Sweetheart…

WYATT

It's one of the best now!

SHARON

You promised to listen.

WYATT breathes deeply and shakes his head.

SHARON (CONT'D)

We have to clarify certain aspects of women's sexuality. The nature of female identity and power. We also have to consult a few more articles and books that are crucial in that area.

WYATT holds his head, fuming.

SHARON (CONT'D)

And then, of course, we have to improve a couple of chapters on the plays themselves.

WYATT groans.

SHARON (CONT'D)

Like… oh, where should I start? How about… *All's Well That Ends Well*?

SHE pats the top of his head. WYATT slowly turns and stares at her in fury.

CURTAIN.

Additional titles from Steele Spring Stage Rights

By VICTOR L. CAHN
Drama | 3F | 80 minutes
A Gripping Political Thriller

Charlotte runs an influential political blog from her home on Cape Cod. Irene, working for a long-time Senator in the midst of a tough campaign, supplies Charlotte with damaging material about the Senator's opponent. Megan, an aide to that opponent, arrives with new reports, and the three power-brokers lock horns in a battle of manipulation and political intrigue. As charges escalate and the battle swerves in unexpected directions, these highly intelligent and articulate women serve up blackmail, power plays, and plenty of media spin. In other words, politics as usual! **"A tight drama, cleverly constructed!"** –New York Theatre Wire

By BETH KANDER | Comedy | 3F, 2M | 95 minutes
"A raucous new comedy!" –Jackson Free Press

Jane's life turns upside down on the worst possible day: the day she decides to quit smoking! When this 30-year old waitress announces to her friends and family that she's quitting "for real," they're supportive. In fact, they're a little bit too supportive. Each has n explosive announcement of their own to share, from a looming divorce to an impending sexual crisis, but nobody wants to be responsible for Jane falling off the non-smoking wagon. As they trip over themselves to keep their secrets secret, who would suspect that Jane is keeping the biggest secret of all? Will Jane quit quitting? This delightful southern comedy proves that you can quit smoking, but you can't quit your crazy family! **"Light-hearted and entertaining—a playful Southern romp!"** –Lexington Herald Leader

www.stagerights.com

Additional titles from Steele Spring Stage Rights

By BRENT HAZELTON | Play with music | 1M | 1 hour 50 minutes

"Liberace! dazzles the eyes and ears." –Thirdcoast Digest

Meet the man behind the grand. *Liberace!* Is a moving and highly entertaining tribute to the performer and musician famous for his charm, glitz, and glamour. On a set reminiscent of his celebrated television program, Liberace relives the highs (and lows) of his prolific life, revealing the real person behind the persona of an enormously talented and acclaimed performer in American history. Interwoven with a rollicking piano score spanning classical and popular music from Chopin to "Chopsticks," and Rachmaninoff to Ragtime, this solo-performer tour de force will have your audience cheering the life of a uniquely American icon.

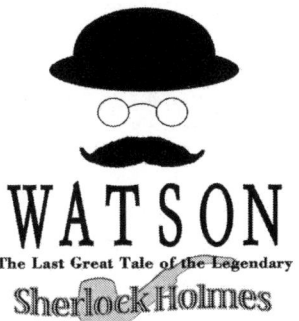

By JAIME ROBLEDO | Comedy | 4F, 7M | 1 hour 45 minutes

"Inventive, epic comedy." –Los Angeles Times

A mystery, a legend, an enduring friendship. *Watson: The Last Great Tale of the Legendary Sherlock Holmes* tells the story of a good man trapped in the shadow of a great man. Funny, moving, and theatrically inventive, this high-energy play balances witty comedy and dramatic mystery to recount the last great tale of the legendary Sherlock Holmes as seen through the eyes of his trusted friend and colleague, Dr. John H. Watson. From pantomime to *Punch and Judy* and with the theatrical ingenuity of Broadway's *The 39 Steps*, *Watson* tells a grand tale of heroes and villains that will captivate your audience until the very end! **"A real crowd pleaser!"** –Backstage

www.stagerights.com

Additional titles from Steele Spring Stage Rights

By BETH KANDER | Drama | 5F | 1 hour, 45 minutes
WINNER of the 2012 Charles M. Getchell New Play Award

Sara is wisecracking, single, broke, and secular. Neshama is serious, married, infertile, and Orthodox. When fate, God, and Sara's Episcopalian roommate bring these two Jewish women together, each must question what really matters, what they really want—and what they're willing to do to get it. As Sara considers donating her eggs, and Neshama ponders accepting them, both women find themselves unexpectedly scrambled. "*Scrambled* is funny, poignant, and relevant to anyone who has ever wondered what they're supposed to be doing with their life. The characters feel familiar, and yet the story feels fresh—a powerful combination."
–Denise Halbach, SETC

Miss Abigail's guide to Dating, Mating, & Marriage!

By KEN DAVENPORT & SARAH SALTZBERG
Comedy | 1F, 1M | 75 minutes

"PURE FUN! You can't help but fall instantly in love with Miss Abigail's Guide!" - *Entertainment Weekly*

Let Miss Abigail take you back to a simpler time, before booty calls and speed-dating, back when the divorce rate wasn't 50% and when 'fidelity' was more than an investment firm! It's *Loveline* meets *Dr. Ruth* as Miss Abigail shares her vast knowledge of every piece of relationship literature known to mankind. The audience participates in this hilarious variety show, and Miss Abigail's strapping young assistant Paco is there to provide for her every need. This smash off-Broadway hit will keep you laughing all night long – that's the Miss Abigail guarantee! **"Big laughs!"** –*Associated Press;* **"Truly a Can't Miss!"** –*Harper's Bazaar*

www.stagerights.com

Additional titles from Steele Spring Stage Rights

Created by C. STEPHEN FOSTER, CHUCK PELLETIER, and ROD DAMER

Musical | 2F, 2M | 90 minutes

"A bright musical with breezy wit and irony." –Los Angeles Times

John, Cliff, Anna, and Divonne live out their complicated lives in the green room of their school's theatre department. Both hilarious and heartwarming, this modern musical gives an authentic account of the struggles these four college theatre majors have in finding their place in the world. The rock-infused pop score includes the Songwriter's Guild of America award-winning song, "It's All About Me." If you've ever been an actor or wanted to be an actor, you'll certainly relate to the Broadway dreams of these characters in this sure-fire hit! **"A surprisingly sweet tale of ambition and talent."** –Sacramento Bee

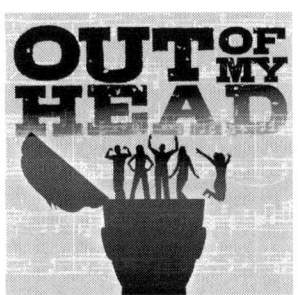

Music and Lyrics by RYAN SCOTT OLIVER

Book by KIRSTEN GUENTHER

Musical | 3F, 2M | 70 minutes

"Sophisticated and impressively clever." –LAist

Out Of My Head is a compelling new musical from Ryan Scott Oliver, recipient of the American Theatre Wing's Jonathan Larson Grant and the prestigious Richard Rodgers Award for Musical Theatre. Five 20-something strangers bare their hearts and souls as they journey through their lives, loves, and losses during a pair of free group therapy sessions. From the moment of their breakdowns to their ultimate breakthroughs, the smart and emotional interplay of these quirky characters brings them all the self-discovery to set aside their insecurities and face the world anew— a little less frightened and a little more brave than before. This fresh and contemporary chamber musical celebrates the amazing strength of the human spirit. **"Witty and provocative."** –Backstage

www.stagerights.com

Additional titles from Steele Spring Stage Rights

by DON GOODRUM
Based on the classic story by Stephen Vincent Benet
Drama | 1F, 5M, Ensemble | 2 hours

A Classic Tale That Proves There Is No Such Thing As A Free Lunch

The devil is known by many names, but we all know that he's not to be trusted, even in one's darkest hour. Jabez, a poor soul who can't seem to catch a break, has hit his personal low when a man named Scratch shows up to offer a deal; seven years of prosperity in exchange for his soul. Jabez takes the deal and his life takes a miraculous turn for the better, that is until it comes time to pay the piper. Now, with his eternal soul hanging in the balance, he hires famed lawyer Daniel Webster to get him out of a contract straight from hell. In a tale that draws as much from an episode of *Law and Order* as it does from history, this is the fight of the century, and one man's life and the future of a nation are at stake. **"A clever re-telling. Charming on every level!"** –Northwest Florida Daily News

by ROB LAUER
Comedy | 2F, 4M, 2 Girls, 2 Boys | 1 Hour, 45 Minutes

Lights! Camera! Prayer!

Journey back to the late 1960s on the television set of *Tom and Penny's Yard Party*: an evangelical show for children on WJIK-TV (Where Jesus Is King). Tom and Penny are a young married couple who broadcast their wholesome "Jesus loves you!" message to living rooms across the country. As the stress of off-camera station politics and the reality of their troubled marriage come to a head, Tom and Penny's world begins to unravel and we see a far less polished side to our bible-thumping hosts. When Penny reads a fan letter from the mother of an odd young boy in the studio audience, everything falls apart–live and on air. **Tune in! This dark comedy of errors is sure to make you a true believer.**

www.stagerights.com

Made in the USA
Middletown, DE
16 July 2015